Waiting for Winter

A Memoir

Elizabeth A. Prost

4TH FLOOR PRESS

www.4thfloorpress.com

©2020 Elizabeth Prost

All rights reserved. No part of this publication may be reproduced in any form or by any means without the express prior written consent of the publisher and/or author, other than short excerpts (200 words or less) for reviews.

THIS BOOK IS COMPRISED OF THE AUTHOR'S PERSONAL MEMORIES, EXPERIENCES, AND INSIGHTS. THIS BOOK IS NOT INTENDED AS A SUBSTITUTE FOR THE MEDICAL ADVICE OF PHYSICIANS. THE READER SHOULD REGULARLY CONSULT A PHYSICIAN IN MATTERS RELATING TO HIS/HER PHYSICAL AND MENTAL HEALTH.

ISBN 978-1-988993-29-4

eISBN 978-1-988993-30-0

eISBN 978-1-988993-31-7

Published by 4th Floor Press, Inc.
www.4thfloorpress.com
1st Printing 2020
Cover Design by Lisa Amoroso
Cover Image iStockphoto.com
Printed in Canada

For Armand and Irene Prost
Allen, Michelle, Charlotte, Lawrence, Mark, David,
and Donnie.

Lizzie Prost

Contents

ACT I
Death — 1
A Parent's Choice — 8
Toronto — 29
Mania. Sex. Love. — 39
Explore the World — 49
Go East Then West — 56
Daisy Duck — 71
Insomnia — 91
Create — 104
Winter — 122

ACT II
Savannah — 141
Home — 161
Love — 165
Breakthrough — 174
Breakdown — 177
Misery — 184

ACT III
Help — 189
Epiphany — 194
Hope & Joy — 199
About the Author — 201

ACT I

Death

This is no rehearsal. When the curtain is down, the show is over

    I was in the truck with the motor running. *How long does it take for carbon monoxide poisoning? Twenty minutes? Half-hour? An hour?* I was trembling and the truck's noise and the rumbling were deafening. I was desperate. I wanted the suffering to end. *How can I go through another depression breakdown?* My mind was reeling. The truck was in the garage and getting hot. It was the middle of summer. I was in my pajamas and it was about three in the afternoon. *Do I really want to die like this?* I left a cry for help note for my partner Donnie on the kitchen table. If I were serious, would I have left a note at all?

Suddenly, I heard a loud "NO!" Donnie rushed into the garage and pulled me out of the driver's seat. He was terrified and furious all at once. I said nothing as I ran into the house and hid in my bedroom. I was ashamed and confused. Did I want to be saved? Probably. I got his attention. "What just happened changes everything for me," he said.

He called my doctor for help. That night, the police showed up on our doorstep and I was taken to the hospital emergency. "Leave me alone, I am okay," I pleaded.

"It is the law, we have to take you in."

All I was interested in was getting sleeping pills. I waited on a bed in a cubicle with curtains. After what seemed to be an eternity, a young doctor came in. I told him that I couldn't sleep and my doctor had stopped the sleeping pills. He did not ask me any questions. I could tell he was in a hurry. He gave me a few pills and I took a taxi home. I could not wait to take a pill to sleep and forget about the horrible events of the day.

Donnie said nothing.

How else do people end their lives? The next day, once again, I was feeling desperate, depressed, and impulsive. I ran down to the basement and found a long cord from Donnie's guitar amplifier. I found a stepping stool and ran outside in my pyjamas, determined to hang myself from a tree branch. I had no idea what I was doing. I tied the cord around the branch and then around my neck. I teetered on the stool and let go. I could feel the tension around my neck *'This is it; I want to end this incessant suffering.'* Suddenly, the cord broke. I fell to the ground and hit my head and, for a moment, I thought I had knocked myself out. My necklace broke and was lying in a bed of pine needles. I felt nothing for it. I ran back into the house and found some string. Again, I tried the tree and stepping stool hanging. Next door, I could hear a lawnmower running. *'Oh my god, what if the neighbour sees me?'* The string was digging into the back of my neck. *'This is ridiculous. I don't want to do this. It's not working anyway.'* I crawled up the tree with my feet and desperately undid the string around my neck. If I had been serious, wouldn't I have found a noose? Where the hell does one get that and how does it work? I kept thinking of the old man from the movie *Shawshank Redemption* and how he did not want to be scared anymore. I understood how he felt. He was by himself in a boarding house room, dressed in a suit, stood on a chair with a noose on his neck, and then, he let go.

My feet were covered in dirt and pine needles. I did not give a damn. I moved the stool and threw the cord back into the basement. I was frustrated and angry with myself. I crawled into bed and hid from the world and tried to forget. Donnie came home at about four o'clock and I didn't say a word.

I wasn't ready to give up on ending it all. Depression, in my experience with or without medication, can last up to a year. A few days later, it was the end of July 2016, the Friday before the long weekend. I looked up "painless suicide" on my cell phone. It said drinking rubbing alcohol would do the trick. I did not know this person I had become. I ran out of the house to my neighbour's house and asked them for rubbing alcohol. I told them I had a cut on my foot. They did not have any. I ran over to Bob and Helen's house on the other side of ours. They were in their eighties and had just lost a son to suicide a year before. Bob found me some rubbing alcohol. I went home and drank half a bottle of it and went to bed to wait for death. I felt sick to my stomach and threw up on the hallway floor.

By this time, it was mid-afternoon, and I heard Donnie coming home. He frantically asked, "What did you do?" I showed him the bottle of alcohol.

"Where are my pills? I need my pills," I kept asking him. I was in bed and I could hear him cleaning up my puke in the hallway outside my bedroom. He sat at the kitchen table struggling with what to do. I kept coming in and out of the kitchen saying, "Please don't call an ambulance, they will institutionalize me!"

"You need help. If you don't call 911, I will." He did and all I could remember was that a heavy hailstorm plummeted the ambulance, me, the first responders, and the road. I tried to fight them and yelled, "Please, I cannot go, please let me out." They held me down and I gave up. I was a young fifty-two-year-old woman in big trouble, and I had been there many times before—too many times to count. On that day, I had been saved from my self- destructive behaviour. I had no idea the nightmare I was about to endure over the next four days. Happy fucking August long weekend to me.

The ambulance took me to the Foothills Hospital in northwest Calgary. I was stuck in a room on a hospital bed with curtains and a male nurse kept coming in and checking my vitals and hooked me up with a saline solution into my arm. Time stood still. I could not think or feel anything except a kind of weird shock. I found my cell phone in my purse and had the energy to text my dear cousin Rob. All I could say was, "I am in the hospital." I had to pee badly, so I pulled the tube out of my arm and blood spewed everywhere on the floor and onto the curtains. I found the bathroom and relieved myself. The male nurse was not pleased. He hooked me up again, then proceeded to clean up the blood on the floor and called someone to change the bloodied curtains.

About an hour later, a female psychiatrist came in and asked me a bunch of questions. She had no compassion for me whatsoever. She seemed impatient and just wanted to get the procedure over with and me out of there. I was so out of it, I cannot for the life of me remember what she asked. I am guessing textbook psychiatrist questions. She did say, "We are going to try you on some different medications."

'Oh no, not this again.'

I replied, "I don't think this is the right time to experiment with new medications."

She replied emphatically, "In the hospital is the right place."

What the hell did she know about medications and psychiatric wards in hospitals? Did she have personal experience? Had she seen family members or friends treated like they were nuts or ignored by psychiatric nurses and doctors? Was she responsible for the misuse and abuse of anti-psychotic drugs by family doctors and psychiatrists in hospitals and old folks' homes? Did she know the reality of mental illness in the city, country, and world? Not bloody likely. I could not think and did not have the energy to stand up for myself and there was no one there to speak on my behalf. *How did I get here?*

A Parent's Choice

Do you lose the child and save the artist?
Do you save the child and lose the artist?
I choose to save the artist and heal the child.

You may think this is going to be a story about winter. Perhaps I am toiling through a cold prairie storm. Or, maybe I am going to describe what snow feels, looks, or tastes like. Perhaps it will be a story of a tremendously gifted figure skater that spends most of her life on ice. Maybe it is a story of death inside an artist. It is not just a story about mental illness, hospitalizations, drugs, and rehabilitation. It is my story. It is as true as can be. What do I have to lose?

I am going to begin on a prairie; a simple, vast, open piece of the world. Life is hard there, but the people are not. I was born in the spring when the leaves were just bursting out. One day, there's nothing and the next, there's a sea of light green on a blue sky that unfolds for the world to see. It seems like a miracle. And then, there is a birth. My five brothers and sisters must have thought "another one?" I am number six in a baseball team of seven, or is it nine? Was this a product of a sexual impulse or a miracle of intention? My mother was all of twenty years old when she had her first baby and said to me not so long ago, "I wanted a baseball team of children." She got her wish.

I was born with a curiosity for the world that, in my eyes, was second to none. I was precocious, "high strung," as my mother would say, and fiery like a thoroughbred colt. I remember the opening sequence to the 1972 show *Black Beauty*. The horse ran freely in an open field as the music soared. At the age of eight, my heart soared.

My mother raised seven children and my father was an entrepreneur and perhaps a jack-of-all-trades. They both were kind, generous, and very hard-working. They were small, like me. Mom and Dad each stood five feet two or so but with the strength and force of an army. They were a formidable little force. My mother and father drew on this strength time and time again to cope with the challenges of living on the prairies and raising a big family.

My mother had slender, delicate hands with lovely natural nails. She had a sweet singing voice that she shared in the Catholic Church choir. She was petite but possessed an inner strength. I inherited her hands and strong disposition. My dad was short, stocky, and strong like a horse. He was a hockey player, baseball player and had tried most sports when he was young.

His nickname was "Yogi," like Yogi Berra, the famous baseball player because he had played back catcher and he was a damned good umpire, too. I inherited his skating legs. When he was in his sixties and I was in my thirties, we went rollerblading together and I skated behind him, noticing that my stride was exactly like his.

When I came into this world, I had skates on my little feet. I loved the ice and snow because it was clean. It was pure and an open palette with infinite possibilities. Gliding across the ice was like floating. It just required a little balance and perhaps some natural talent. My father taught me to skate at the age of four. I followed him on the ice like a duckling to a duck. "Push with both feet," he said, "not just with one."

'Good idea,' I thought, *'Why push around on just one skate when I can use both?'* My legs were getting sore and I thought it might balance me out, too.

In the living room of the first house we lived in, I danced and pranced with the beautiful sounds of my mother's classical records. At the time, the room was big and long and I was small but fierce with the desire to dance. *Oh, dearest mother, what to do with this little bundle of talent? What dreams do you have in mind? Are they yours or are they hers?*

Between the ages of four to six, it was my way or the highway, although, my mother would have thought otherwise. All I would eat was Lipton's Chicken Noodle Soup. Shaking my head adamantly, I would say, "Nope, chicken noodle soup, chicken noodle soup." I was a precocious child and liked to boss my little brother David around. We built forts and igloos together. I would play dress-up and pretend I was an actress in a movie. I asked my brother in a dramatic voice, "How do I look?"

He replied, "Gross." I slapped him across the face like a diva. My dad slapped me across the bottom. My older sister Charlotte yelled, "She has got a hand-print on her bum!" By grade one, this would all change.

I knew who I was on the first day of school. Sitting in my desk near the front, I looked up and down at the rows of boys and girls in my class and asked myself, *'This is it? This is my class?'* From that moment on, I knew deep down that I was different. And my life would prove to be not only non-conventional but extraordinary.

Being hopeful and making the best of any situation, I settled into a routine. In the town that I grew up in, there wasn't much to do except school, skating, and exploring the town and fields. So, every day, my schedule looked like this: skating, school, skating, repeat. But, then, of course, there were three meals a day at home with my family. That took up a great deal of time. There were nine, you see, including my mom and dad. My mother was a good cook and we ate very well. With six siblings around the table, I ate what was on my plate. There was no negotiation. Not like nowadays where parents ask questions like, "What would you like to eat? How about five different choices?" Good luck with that. I remember my mother saying, "Quality time is a joke. It is ALL the time."

By the age of seven, my mother had another activity in mind—piano lessons. I was sent to the town's piano teacher, in a church, to learn the basics. The teacher, from what I could tell, could play by ear and read music. She learned to read music and had a keen ear.

Low and behold, a piano arrived at our home in all its glory. It was big and beautiful. Mother was proud. And so, it all began—eleven years of practice and proficiency with the pianoforte. At the end of it, I received the prestigious honour of Grade Eight Royal Conservatory of Music. But, I jump ahead. Let's backtrack, shall we?

Back to the hub of the town: the skating rink. My dad helped build that monstrosity with beams normally reserved for the construction of a cathedral. They curved into an arch. How does wood bend like that? For years, that rink had natural ice with a hand flooder and hand scrapers. There was no Zamboni in sight until the eighties.

Oh, how can I describe natural ice? It shines and glows like dew on the grass in the morning light. It is pure, soft, and smells delicious, like fresh spring rain. At just the right temperature and softness under the blade, it feels like gliding on a cloud. It is effortless. At the wrong temperature, it bangs and cracks in all different directions. It is hard, slick, and the palette of lines almost disappear in one stroke, especially if one weighs a mere eighty pounds.

I remember Saturday mornings the most. My dad would drive to the rink at seven in the morning and pick me up at ten. He always came back early to watch the free skate. I liked that. Oh, to have my father watch me with such unconditional love and admiration. I have met no other man like him. I skated my heart out and learned all about the art of the edge. I remember the bench in the waiting room where Dad helped me lace the skates. He had stronger hands than me. "Are they tight enough?"

"Yes," was always my answer.

I remember music playing like Waldteufel's *Skater's Waltz* and Elton John's *Crocodile Rock*. We sometimes played old records on the turntable in the music room and occasionally made prank phone calls, thinking no one would hear us.

My first coach was Joanne Frank. She was fiery and got things done in the little town. Figure skating played second fiddle to hockey and she fought for ice time. She somehow managed, in her not so subtle ways, to nurture her students' creativity. Mrs. Frank was one of the few coaches that had this gift. I won my first bronze medal at the age of ten. I was a little spark plug with skinny legs attached. I remember driving home in a storm. I felt warm, safe, and secure in the backseat with my medal around my neck. I couldn't wait to show it to my mom and dad. Joanne dropped off a couple of skaters at their farm and then we made it home safe and sound. For a child, a storm is exciting and not scary at all. For the driver, it is another story altogether. The snow drifted across the road on the tail of the wind. It danced in all directions in front of the car lights. A sea of white on black where one could not differentiate the road from the ditch. I remember Dad, on several occasions, would open the door and watch for the yellow line on the highway. And, sometimes we would pull over somewhere safe to wait it out. Snowstorms, in all their glory and drama, shall pass and end in a drift.

Those years as a child in Radville, Saskatchewan passed quickly and unceremoniously. The town and fields were our playgrounds in every season. My four brothers always seemed to keep things lively. They played hockey, drove cars, chased girls, and managed to stay out of trouble for the most part. My eldest brother Allen drove race cars. He was like a rockstar to me and our younger brother David. We tagged along with the middle siblings to a track outside of town. It was entertaining and exciting, to say the least. Allen was a good driver. I don't remember him being around too much. It was tough being the oldest of seven children. I sensed that he couldn't wait to get the hell out of dodge. I remember the day he left in his little sports car. Go west, young man, and build a life. And so, he did. He ended up in Kamloops, British Columbia. And, there he would remain.

My older brother Mark was considered the black sheep of the family, although he was the kindest and most generous. He quit Radville High School in grade nine because the teachers were idiots. He hung out in our dad's garage. Mark's eyes were glued to Yogi and the day-to-day business of running a garage. He also had his eye on his little skating sister who he affectionately called "Poo Bear." He coined that nickname when we were watching Winnie the Poo and I asked quizzically, "What's a poo?" In the years that followed, Mark pulled all kinds of shenanigans including "borrowing" the station wagon with a local chic and heading south to god knows where. A guardian angel must have been following him around because he managed to stay alive. When he was much older, Mark checked himself into rehab for addiction to drugs. When he was there, he said to his counsellors, "Tell me what to do. I will do whatever it takes." This was to be his most important month of learning in all of his life. Radville High School could kiss his ass. So long suckers.

My eldest sister Michelle was a babysitter for most of her teenage life. She took care of the horde and perhaps was frustrated with her lot in life. My older sister Charlotte looked like an innocent little angel. She watched over her little sister from day one and beyond. She got blamed for most of my shenanigans as a child. I was about five years old and wanted some milk so I stood on a stool in front of the fridge and proceeded to lift out a big glass container. It fell and shattered. I jumped off the stool and cut my big toe. Dad came home and was not pleased. "Jesus Christ, who was watching her?"

One Sunday morning, while the house was still asleep, Charlotte instructed me to fetch the play dishes from inside the shelf of their old ironing board that pulled out of the wall. The ironing board fell on my head. I was taken to the hospital for stitches. Who was responsible? While Charlotte was washing dinner dishes, looking out the kitchen window, daydreaming about boys, I climbed up on the counter in my pajamas and proceeded to eat a whole bottle of baby aspirin. I was all of four years old. What was Charlotte daydreaming about? Did she not see her little sister on the counter two feet away from her? I was taken to the hospital to get my stomach pumped. It took a team of doctors and nurses to hold me down. My sister was blamed for all of these unfortunate events. Mother and Father were not pleased.

The town was getting too small for me, a blossoming little bundle of talent. My parents thought, "What are we going to do with her now?" Joanne Frank took me to my first summer skating school in Regina, Saskatchewan. This was the big time for a ten-year-old. I remember being frustrated with figures. The main word in figure skating is figure, which means a practice of going around and around relentlessly in circles. I did not want to stay within the lines. Please let me free skate. And, so began the love and hate relationship with a sport that consumed most of my life.

I missed my mom and dad terribly. So, every weekend, I would go home and sleep in front of a fan on a rug between their two twin beds. Somehow, I felt connected to them with the fan whirring and they on either side of me. I felt comforted, warm, and safe.

That comfort did not last long. *"I am calling on all angels to walk me through this world and not leave me alone because I am not sure how this all goes."* When I needed to cry, this heartbreaking song by Jane Siberry would be at my side. We are not there yet.

At the age of thirteen, I left my home in Radville. Mom and I lived in an apartment within walking distance of the rink in a small city fifty kilometres from Radville. There, I could get the coaching and training I needed. Weyburn's arena had artificial ice. It had some of the best ice that I had ever known. I was in grade nine and attended a junior high school. At five in the morning, I walked to the rink. I remember being so tired at times that I thought of crawling into a snowbank to sleep. After a second breakfast, my mother would drive me to school. She picked me up for lunch, drove me back to school, and then to the rink. Repeat. Of course, there was piano practice in the basement of a lonely church. In the evenings, there was dinner and homework. This continued until Friday when Mom and I would venture back home. This was not before Mom treated me to a Peanut Buster Parfait at the local Dairy Queen. Alas, I was saved. Sunday evening came all too soon and back we went to the city.

My mother looked so sad in that lonely little apartment. I will never forget her sitting in a rocking chair in front of the television with a sad, sullen look on her face. It broke my heart. I was thirteen years old and did not know how to help. We were both trapped in our fate. Oh dear, that hurt so deeply, down to the core of my being. Fortunately, that feeling would pass.

Mom stayed with me for a season. Then, I lived with a series of older, widowed women. To this day, I'm not sure how my parents even found those ladies. They took really good care of me. They made meals for me and were good company. In a way, perhaps I took care of them. I still have a soft spot for the elderly.

I ventured into my high school years at the age of fifteen. I was in my prime as a skater. My body was small, fast, lean, and I could jump like a rabbit. I was like a little, fiery sports car. I believed there was nothing I could not do. Boys did not interest me in the least. The junior hockey team practised right after the figure skating and I did everything in my power to show off how fast I could skate and how high I could jump. Their eyes were on my every move. Although, what do hockey players think about?

The year flew by because I was so very busy. My schedule continued to look pretty much the same. There were two hours of skating in the wee hours of the morning, followed by school, nap, and lunch; continuing with more school, two more hours of skating, dinner, piano practice, homework, and bed. I didn't particularly enjoy high school politics but I did love school. I was very clever and studious. My favourite subjects were biology, English, history, and gym. The eighty and ninety percentiles came quite easily. My world revolved around a three-kilometre radius in the small city. The rink, school, and piano lessons.

Home became my weekend refuge. Friday nights, I would collapse on the couch, watch television with my dad, and fall asleep before ten o'clock. Dad retired to bed and there I stayed until I woke up at around midnight and stumbled sleepily to my room. Saturday nights, I would fall asleep to the comforting sounds of *Hockey Night in Canada* on the television. By that time, it was just me and my younger brother David at home. The rest of our siblings were scattered around the countryside. I don't remember them much. Even my little brother seemed to have lost touch. The weekend flew by much too fast and then it was Sunday. How could I hold onto the day? In the evening, Mom or Dad would drive me back to Weyburn. Mom had clean clothes ready and muffins for the morning. Every week, my heart sank. I felt deflated and alone. I'm sure they felt the same way. But, there was nothing else to do.

Are you asking yourself, "What was all of this training for?" This is a good question that I asked myself, too. Well, there needs to be a performance or two. Every year, I performed at the provincial level in the Jean Norman Competition and Sectionals. Dad drove me all over Saskatchewan to small cities like Swift Current, Moosejaw, Saskatoon, and Regina to compete in them. There were no figures in those events, just free skating. I did very well and won a few. However, the most important award I received was the Amy Award. The small silver plate read, "Amy Award—Most Artistic Skater."

At the Jean Norman, there were no figures; just free skate. Those blasted figures. What is the point of going around in circles over and over again to trace edges one on top of the other? Simply, some of the best skaters in the world did figures. They are like scales to a piano player. I liked the meditative aspect of them. Technically, they are invaluable. Artistically, they can crush creativity. Imagine me, with my skinny little legs, standing on a bare piece of ice with seven or so judges scrutinizing my every move. My whole body shook and, because I was so light, I could barely see the tracings. Bigger girls with big hips are good at figures. Overall, I despised them. I remember a story of an international skater named Gary Beacom who took his "figure" skates and threw them in a garbage can after the "figure" part of the competition. Yes, we had separate skates for Figures and Free skate. The former had no lower toe pick and a different sharpening. The latter had huge toe picks for jumping and a deeper edge. Beacom was an incredibly gifted artistic skater. I wished I could have expressed my anger and frustration in such a dramatic manner—but

I never did.

Provincial Sectionals and Western Canadian Divisionals were a different story. From fifteen to eighteen years old, I started as a Novice and finished as a Junior Ladies skater. Figures were my nemesis. They were the first third of the competition. I always placed at the bottom of the pack. That determined where you started for the second part of the competition which was the short program. That was at the beginning when the judges withheld their marks for the later flights of skaters. I performed well but never enough to reach the top. I thought, "What's the point?" It all seemed barbaric to me.

Nothing was ever good enough. There was always a push for perfection. It's an illusion that does not exist, except in nature. Sadly, I don't remember my coaches or parents ever telling me I was a beautiful skater. Was that "old school" teaching or parenting? For years, my internal monologue was "I am not good enough" because that was all I knew. However, one Saskatchewan judge said to me, "I love to watch you skate." Ellen Burka, a renowned Torontonian coach yelled out, "*J'adore!*" after I had completed a beautiful double Lutz with my arms over my head. It is uncanny how we hold onto a glimpse of approval or applause of any kind.

When I was sixteen, I had an extremely good and

tough coach named Fred. Because we had to compete with the hockey teams for ice time, he rented ice at the old Regina Coliseum at two in the morning. It smelt like an old barn because it was next to the exhibition grounds. Even my sweater smelt like cows after I hung it on the boards. Imagine doing mind-numbing figures at that hour. During free skate, Fred made me do my long program twice in a row. Afterwards, I felt like throwing up.

Fred was gay and lived with one of his students named Ernie. One day, I was over at his home trying out pair skating lifts in his indoor pool with Ernie. Fred made it clear to me and my parents that, "Elizabeth is not going to make it as a single skater with her figures. She and Ernie should compete as a pair."

'Oh my god,' I thought, *'here is my chance…no more figures…enough of staying in the lines. I could be saved!'*

My parents did not go for it. They said, "We have enough trouble just worrying about you, let alone having someone else in the picture." They did not completely trust Fred and wanted me to complete my Gold Figure Level. That was the highest test that you could pass in the Canadian figure skating system. That was it. I was completely deflated, defeated, and heartbroken. I cried and hung my head. I knew deep down that I was talented enough to make it to the Canadians, Worlds, or even the Olympics as a pair skater. However, I was destined to be a single skater—a lonely artist carving my blades into a sheet of white ice and then turning the blade onto myself.

For the next three years, my heart wasn't really into it. At times, I became sullen and depressed. Most of the time, I never showed it. I just went through the motions, day after day and year after year. Occasionally, I would act out. I never was great with expressing anger, but I remember a few times swearing at my skates and coach in frustration. I should have taken my "figure" skates and thrown them clear across the ice. But, I did not and I forged on.

My skating buddy in Weyburn, Saskatchewan was David Nickel. He was an amazing talent. He was my good friend and he was like a brother to me. That part of the world was getting too small for him, too. Off he went to Toronto and my heart sank, but not for long. In the summer, I followed him to Toronto and had some of the best times of my life. We trained at the infamous Toronto Cricket Skating and Curling Club. It was home to some of the best skaters in the world, including Toller Cranston, Tracy Wilson and Rob McCall, Tracey Wainman, just to name a few. It was also home to some of the best coaches in Canada including Ellen Burka, Osborne Colson, Sheldon Galbraith, and Donald Jackson. Ellen Burka coached Toller Cranston, Sheldon Galbraith coached Barbara Anne Scott, and

Osborne Colson coached me! I was at home at the club because I was with my peers and good friends. Oh, what a time we had. We skinny-dipped in the club pool, drank alcohol on the subway, had outdoor parties in the city forest where the nunnery was, hung out at the mall downtown, and made complete fools of ourselves in public and at house parties. I was all of sixteen years old. Did I mention that we skated for six hours a day?

We practised figures and free skate one session after another. I think I got high off the Zamboni fumes. The days were full but the sultry summer nights in Toronto were our own to do with whatever pleased us. I have such wonderful memories of seasons in Toronto. It was sad to leave the big city and go back to Weyburn, Saskatchewan. I felt very much alone there. Thankfully, I had some good friends in Radville. My dear cousin Rob was like a brother to me. To this day, he is my pillar of strength and war buddy. Have I mentioned the war? We are not there yet.

Rob and I had hung out since I was about four years old. He was another closeted gay teenager, which must have been difficult in a small town like Radville. For reasons that I cannot begin to explain, Rob has battled depression his whole life. He was, and still is, the most sensitive, generous, and kind person I have ever known. Perhaps not to himself, but there it is.

We did get into some trouble in our younger years. When my dad's mother Agnes died of an aneurysm in her sixties, my cousin and I had to bring up the water and wine at a Roman Catholic funeral. We sat in the pews waiting patiently through the service. Right beside us, an elderly man fell asleep and bumped his forehead on the hardwood pew in front of him. Rob and I got the giggles that wouldn't stop. People glared at us as we stifled laughter on our way up the church aisle. The statue of the body of Christ nailed to the cross at the front of the church alter should have been looking down on us with Mona Lisa's smile.

One of my fondest memories as a teenager in skating was participating in the Canada Winter Games in Brandon, Manitoba in 1976. I was part of a team of athletes from Saskatchewan and was so very proud. I remember staying in the athlete's village and feeling so grown up. There was a disco dance floor with the music of Rod Stewart filling the room. I had my first teenage crush and kiss. I met a weightlifter from Quebec. We hung out and ended up kissing outside the food hall. I fantasized about him for months after. I did not win a medal but I skated fairly well. During the closing ceremonies, the athletes exchanged outfits. I traded my Saskatchewan white and green parka for a blue Quebec outfit. It was an exciting time for a young athlete like me. My parents came to watch and drove me back home. I rested in the back of the station wagon and fantasized about winning a medal at a major competition. Driving home with Mom and Dad made me feel safe and secure.

In the summer of 1981, I had my first serious skating injury. I was on a free skating session, performing my long program. I was skating backwards, then turned forward with my right leg and collided with the back of a girl's wicked free leg blade right into the flesh of my knee. I saw my leg split open, feel down, and immediately covered the gash with my hands. Everyone on the ice gathered around me and I heard someone yell out, "Is there a doctor in the building?" Remarkably, there was. They carried me to a bench and the doctor had to pry my hands off my knee. I looked up at the crowd around me and saw them grimace and turn away. I thought, *'This is not good.'* An ambulance took me away. I was in shock and did not feel any pain. At the hospital, the nurses shot me up with Demerol and I slurred my words to the physician saying, "Please sew me up good, Doc." I had forty stitches in three layers.

David Watson was another good skating buddy of mine. Mrs. Watson (bless her heart) offered to take me into her home to take care of me for a few days until I could fly home. I called Mom and Dad in bed with my leg propped up and told them what had happened. My mom was so upset she said, "Talk to your dad." The first night was a piece of cake because I was on Tylenol 3s. When they wore off, my leg was throbbing and felt like it had separated from my body. The girl who had skated into me visited and brought gifts of flowers and a new pair of leggings because my other ones were trashed. I believe she felt bad about what happened.

I, however, did not feel so bad. I had the opportunity to go home and be looked after by my mom. I laid out on the back deck of our house in Radville, overlooking the garden with my leg propped up. Mom made me good food and took me to my doctor and physio appointments. Now, I think of Red Pollard and Sea Biscuit. I needed time to heal and, in a way, I was saved.

It took several weeks for my leg to heal. At one point, my knee was swollen. My mom took me to the doctor, and he proceeded to squeeze this grossly coagulated dark blood out of my wound. My mom had to look away. After a month, physio helped but I had lost most of the muscle mass on my leg.

I went back to Weyburn in the fall and did a great deal of physiotherapy. For the next two years, I became more and more sad and lonely. I think I was a depressed kid who didn't know what to do about that.

Toronto

An athlete. Aim higher, stronger, faster.
An artist. Inspiration and risk.
Setting and peer group is key.

When I was sixteen years old, my comrade, David Nickel, moved to Toronto to train with the renowned Ellen Burka at the Toronto Cricket Skating and Curling Club. I was heartbroken and deflated. I was left to skate with young skaters who generally pissed me off because they would dilly dally around the ice. It was no one's fault. I was stuck in Weyburn getting a good education, excellent piano training but I had no one at my level to skate with for five hours a day. I had spent summer schools in Lethbridge, Alberta; Saskatoon and Regina, Saskatchewan; but nothing compared to the atmosphere of the Cricket Club.

It was founded in 1827 by George Anthony Barber. The Toronto Curling Club was organized in 1836 and the Toronto Skating Club was officially founded in 1895. The amalgamation of three of Toronto's oldest clubs, including the Toronto Cricket Club, happened in 1957. The official name Toronto Cricket and Skating

Club was a result of a 25-cent coin toss at a meeting at the Royal Ontario Museum. This is all interesting, but we always knew it as the Cricket Club.

In the late 1970s, it was a somewhat hoity-toity private club situated on the south side of Wilson Avenue near the York Mills Subway Station. It was home to famous figure skaters from several generations like Barbara Anne Scott, Petra Burka, Osborne Colson, Toller Cranston, Dorothy Hamill, Tracy Weinman, and Patrick Chan. It had a beautifully manicured Cricket field, indoor and outdoor swimming pools, curling rink, and a beautiful (no boards) skating rink. There were mirrors and windows at one end and a glassed-in viewing area at the other.

I followed in David's footsteps at the age of seventeen. I attended summer school at the Cricket Club and I still remember the mid-century carpets, an antique wooden staircase, the smells of sanitized locker rooms and Zamboni fumes off a freshly flooded ice surface. I also remember the smell of Toronto's humid summer air and the fresh dew as I walked across the large Cricket field every morning.

I made friends easily and soon was nicknamed "Dizzy Lizzie" because I would skate so hard, come off the ice in a daze, and sit in the viewing area until I could see straight. My best friends were David Nickel and Dianne Stewart. She was as nutty and good-humoured as I was. She and David kept me somewhat sane as we trained seven hours a day for two months. They also dated before he came out of the closet. I think they were just particularly good friends. I always joked about turning men gay. The truth was, they were gay to begin with. In 1979, it was not accepted — even in the figure skating world.

Dianne was an ace at figures. She could trace figure eights, rockers, counters, brackets, and loops like there was no tomorrow. Sounds like I am talking about hardware equipment. No, those are twists and turns on circles repeatedly until you get in a weirdly meditative state or go completely crazy. I experienced both the former and the latter with a little frustration thrown in. I wanted to free skate with jumps, spins, footwork, edges of art to music and everything in between.

My coach was Osborne "Ozzie" Colson who won the 1936 and 1937 Canadian Championships. I remember seeing a black and white photo of him in a suit performing in a 1940s ice show with a live orchestra. Through the 1920s to 1950s, shows were like the *Ziegfeld Follies* on ice. Fannie Brice and Esther Williams eat your heart out. In America, it was the *Ice Capades* — "The Greatest Show on Earth."

Mr. Colson was as gay as the day was long. To be honest, most figure skaters are. I couldn't care less at the time because being with gay men was as normal to me as breathing. The important thing was he was an incredible coach. He taught me footwork sequences that blew my mind. He had an ear for music as did I, and helped me choreograph programs to be extremely proud of. He wore a signature cap and coat with style and flair. He was forthright but fair and gave credit when it was due. However, he and many coaches of his time and beyond, could not teach the double axel properly—my other nemesis. It is technically one of the most difficult jumps to orchestrate and complete cleanly. Kurt Browning could do double and triple axels in his sleep. However, in the short program at the 1994 Olympics, he fell performing a double axel. He never medaled at an Olympics but had four World Championship titles under his belt. Maybe the Olympics were his nemesis.

    I fell again and again with that jump and paid for it physically and emotionally later in life. The ice was as unforgiving as the judges at competitions. I thought I wasn't a great skater because I could not do the double axel properly. In my dreams, I performed it perfectly. The truth is, I was a beautiful skater. Unfortunately, I didn't figure that out until I was in my thirties. When people ask me "Do you still skate?" I respond with a smile and point to my head replying, "All I need to do is close my eyes." I'm also reminded of it every time I see my chiropractor.

I spent two glorious summers at the Cricket Club. My skating buddies and I would ride the subway to the Eaton Center, the waterfront, the CN tower, and back again on the Yonge Line to York Mills station. We snuck booze on the subway, went up the CN tower late in the evening, and crashed a nightclub at the top. We snuck in a strange kind of back door to avoid the bouncers. We skinny-dipped after midnight in the outdoor pool at the Cricket Club and went to parties pulling all kinds of shenanigans.

I boarded at one elderly lady's place after another, all within walking distance of the Cricket Club. The first one was an older lady who was quite frail and didn't talk much. She made me a lot of canned tomato soup and grilled cheese sandwiches. One day, after I took a shower, I walked into the kitchen for something and the floor was wet from my feet. While I was at the rink, she slipped and fell. I felt bad about that. I didn't stay there long.

The next lady was kind, wise, and a good cook. She introduced me to peanut butter, onion, and tomato sandwiches. I think my dad would like those sandwiches with a little bacon thrown in. I had a room with a fan to keep me company and lull me to sleep. I also liked the walk in the early morning across the cricket fields while there was still dew on the grass and a faint fog in the air. Toronto in summer had a lovely smell of morning humidity.

I stayed at the Stewarts' home during my last season in Toronto. Dianne's mom was strict with her and quite liberal with me. She was always concerned with Dianne's weight as some figure skating moms can be. I remember Dianne living on carrots and celery most of the time. How the hell did she have the energy to skate seven hours a day? Dianne also worked downtown part-time, perhaps orchestrated by her mom to keep her out of trouble. Of course, in a subtle rebellion, we did our best to find mischief. Being from Saskatchewan, my drink of choice was Southern Comfort and Tab. I can't remember what Dianne drank. We snuck our booze on the subway and brought it to parties. Sometimes, we would stay out until two in the morning, just in time to catch transit home. Dianne got up early and I slept in. I wonder what Mrs. Stewart thought about that?

In the fall, after my knee injury, I went back to Weyburn Comprehensive High School on crutches. I was living with the Greggorys at the time. They didn't have the time of day for me. I think Mrs. Greggory liked the boarding money. Her daughter Heather was my age and was a royal bitch. Maybe she was jealous or resented me in some way. She had a boyfriend and a choice group of friends. For some odd reason, they never invited me to any of their parties. Heather and her boyfriend threw a Halloween party dressed as matching bumble bees. I was in the basement and they never even noticed me sitting on the couch by myself. I called Dad and cried into the phone. He didn't know what to say. I desperately missed my friends in Toronto, especially Dianne and David.

At the end of September, when my leg had nearly healed, I flew back to Toronto to continue where I had left off with my coach. I was tentative and a little scared on the ice. Mr. Colson said, "You got to get back on the horse." I did my best, but I was also in a lot of pain when I pushed it. I took regular excursions to physiotherapy treatments, doing the same routine every time. They used ultrasound to break up the scar tissue, followed by a series of exercises. One time, I saw Frank Augustine, the National ballet dancer. Another time, I saw Ken Read from the Crazy Canucks World Cup alpine ski racers. I must have been at a decent physio clinic.

I stayed in Toronto at Dianne's home for two weeks. Mr. Colson and I finished my short and long programs. Two days before I left, I bought chocolates for Mr. C. and cards for my Torontonian friends. Dianne gave me a sweet little journal as a going-away gift. On the first page, she wrote, "To Dizzy Lizzy, may moments fill your diary. A friend forever, Dianne."

Thirty-five years later, I still have that precious journal and I recently reconnected with Dianne on Facebook. But, I digress.

My skating buddies and I went out the night before I left Toronto. We mixed rum and Tabs at the bus stop and had a riot on the subway—as in fun. We went up to the CN tower to a nightclub called Sparkles. We couldn't get in because most of us had runners on. We were underage as well. While we were up there, I decided to take some photos of the city lights and the moon shining on Lake Ontario. We heard some loud music and saw a door that said, "do not enter." We entered anyway and walked right onto the Sparkles' dance floor. We danced our asses off until midnight and then took the elevator back down the tower. We jumped onto the subway and met a Scottish guy with a strong accent. He didn't know quite where he was going. For some crazy reason, we told him we were bi-sexual. He thought we were all very strange.

We decided to find a place for a snack. We ended up at a place called The Truck Stop that looked like Mel's Diner. It was a real dive with punk people inside—it was 1981 after all. Suddenly, it was 1:45 in the morning and we were going to miss the subway. Coincidentally, one of our friends saw a couple that she babysat for. They were kind enough to give us all a ride home.

On the last day of my Toronto reunion, I had two things left to do: give gifts and attend a going-away party. I gave chocolates and cards to Mr. Colson and the Stewarts. "Ozzie" was tickled pink and Dianne's mom and dad were appreciative. I am sure they weren't appreciative of Dianne going to a crazy figure skater party but there it is. We drank rum and cokes. I didn't drink too much because I wanted to keep my wits about me. We played caps and a game called "What Would You Do If..." Dianne kept running around taking photos. A few of us went into the bathroom to read the "What Would You Do If..." notes. Jack, one of our skating buddies, leaned against the sink and it fell right off the wall. Water was squirting everywhere! Jack got soaked trying to turn the taps off. Finally, someone turned the water off from downstairs. There were two inches of water on the floor and a real mess. The host of the party was upset but we all thought it was crazily funny.

The next morning, I slept through seven a.m. alarm and Dianne woke me up at 8:15 am. We nearly shit bricks! She said, "I have never seen you move so fast." I secretly left a card in one of her bedroom drawers. Luckily, I was pretty much packed. Mrs. Stewart gave us a ride down to the Cricket Club to get my skates and tapes. We made it to the subway station just in time for the 9 a.m. airport shuttle bus. I hated saying goodbye to Dianne. She gave me a gift that I opened on the bus. She gave me a little heart with a candle in it. I balled my eyes out. What an incredibly depressing bus ride. I made it to the terminal with ten minutes to spare.

Home in Radville, I went back to my lonely and repetitive weekly routine of driving to Weyburn on a Sunday night, staying with a family that I did not care for, and skating with a bunch of kids that I had nothing in common with. Because of my injury, I wanted to quit but did not. Before a Western Divisional competition, my dad massaged my legs for me like he used to do when I was a young girl. I desperately wanted to say, "Dad, I am not having fun anymore." But, I did not. I restrained and stifled my voice. Once again, I didn't want to disappoint him or mom, skating and track coaches, my piano teacher, or anyone for that matter. But, at least I had my friends, colleagues, and bountiful memories of Toronto. Who would have known that someday, sooner than later, I would return there for entirely different reasons? Maybe Toronto was my second home away from home in body, mind, and definitely... in spirit.

Mania. Sex. Love.

Manic energy.
Sexual energy.
Love – abundant energy.

I retired from amateur skating right after high school and moved to Regina, Saskatchewan intending to attend university. Out of the blue, I received a call from Dianne who was teaching skating in the mountains of Northern Italy called Piazzatorre. It is a gorgeous ski resort with hotels and semi-open skating rink nestled in the mountains seventy kilometers northeast of Milan and thirty-five kilometres north of Bergamo. She was leaving for the summer and they needed a replacement skating coach. How could I say no? It was Italy!

I was nineteen years old, had no teaching experience, and had just been turned loose from the rigours of amateur training. I wasn't nearly ready, but I made the journey anyway. I remember stepping off the plane onto the stairs of the tarmac and smelling Italy for the first time. It was warm, humid, and delicious. The Pugliese family that hired me and paid my way greeted me at the airport and we drove to Bergamo. They didn't speak much English, but we got the gist of each other. I was to stay with them for a few days before we went to the mountain resort.

I was a wild child. In a few short days, I managed to stay out late into the night riding on the back of motorcycles with Italian boys. I met a nice couple who became my tour guides and we drove around the beautifully quaint small city rich in history and sixteenth-century architecture. There were the Venetian Walls, the Piazza Vecchia, and the church/mausoleum Cappella Colleoni. I didn't have a camera or journal at the time, so I barely remember the city. I do, however, remember my energy. I was vibrating at a whole other frequency—different from athletic energy. Was I manic? Maybe.

Mr. Pugliese drove me to the rink in the mountains to show me around. It was a quintessential mountain resort setting. I went for a skate in the lovely arena, wearing a revealing dress and showing off my skills. Was I a show skater or a coach? I was neither at that moment in time. I was twenty years old for god's sake and had just found my freedom.

Dianne was travelling at the time and I decided to meet her in Southern France. We met at the Nice train station. Nice is genuinely nice. We spent plenty of time at topless beaches. Dianne was nearly as nutty as I was. We were both exploring the world and our sexuality that had been repressed for years in a rink. Dianne continued her travels as I continued to act crazy.

The Pugliese family decided that I was too immature for the job and sent me packing. Later in life, I joked about being "deported from Italy." At the time, I just shrugged it off and made a stopover in Toronto with no idea of where I was going to live or work. I ended up staying with some old skating buddies from a couple of years before. I camped out on their floors for several weeks and wandered the streets of Toronto to the wee hours of the mornings.

I found an out of the way nightclub on Sherbourne Street called The Diamond Club. It had a huge dance floor, stage, and upper-level people-watching area. It has been described as "straight-out-of-New-York-ghetto-chic." One night, I spotted John Candy entertaining some bystanders. The Diamond was also frequented by other comedians like Martin Short and Andrea Martin. Awesome bands like the Tragically Hip, Blue Rodeo, Cowboy Junkies, Martha and the Muffins, and the Jeff Healy Band played there. In 1987, David Bowie played a live midday broadcast on Much Music as a teaser for his *Glass Spider Tour*. The Diamond was called the crown jewel of the late eighties Toronto nightlife. I went there to dance to crowd-pleasers like

Tears for Fears, Prince, and Madonna. I loved to dance by myself for hours on end. I had energy to burn. I was used to training four hours a day in the fall and winter plus seven hours a day at summer schools. When that ended, my body said, "Now what?"

I tried to find a skating teaching job but to no avail. At one point, I decided that I could be a stand-in for movies. I was on a set for a movie called *Head Office* with Danny DeVito and Jane Seymour. One morning, I heard a film assistant yell out, "Is there anyone here four foot eleven?" I looked around and then thought to myself, *'Heh, that's me.'* I introduced myself and ended up being Danny DeVito's stand-in for a day. Wow, what a hoot that was. He was hilarious and full of energy like me. Another time, I skulked out a hockey movie set called *Youngblood* with Rob Lowe, Ed Lauter, and Patrick Swayze. I ended up chatting with Ed Lauter in a tent and stalked Rob Lowe who was trying to play out hockey scenes. I leisurely stood by one of the assistants and noticed on her clipboard what hotel he was staying at. One night, I shamelessly went to his hotel room to do what? I don't know. He opened the door and I said, "Hi, I was at the rink this week watching you skate."

"I am sorry—on the phone right now," he said. It must have been Melissa Gilbert because he was dating her at the time.

I walked the streets of Yorkville, Yonge Street, and Queen Street West day and night. The summers in Toronto are hot, humid, and sultry. I also went to the Eaton Center, downtown to visit David who worked at Mr. Green Jeans. For some odd reason, I had developed a taste for shoplifting. I walked out of a women's clothing store with a black wool dress. The next time was in a drugstore and decided I needed eyeliner. I took one or two and got caught. I was arrested for theft under two hundred dollars. I was placed in the back of a police car on Yonge Avenue right in front of the Eaton Center. I thought it was all a joke and that irritated the police officers. However, after being questioned and fingerprinted, I knew it was serious. That was the end of my petty crime spree.

I finally managed to get a skating job and went to live with a nice gal. I was still on a high that wouldn't quit. The good news was I had settled down a bit. I was on the subway once and wrote my mom a long letter. I have no idea what I said. She did not appreciate it. I went to court for my shoplifting and decided that I was going to be either a lawyer or a writer. I also thought to myself, '*I am going to write a book someday called Waiting for Winter.*' I'm not sure why. The title just came to me. Consciously or perhaps unconsciously, I was waiting for something. I was waiting for the darkness and pain to go away. I was waiting for my life to unfold as it should.

Eventually, I ran out of money and friends to stay with. I ended up at a wayward home for teenagers and women. A girl that I was rooming with seemed like she did not belong there whatsoever. She told me that her father was a lawyer and was abusive. There were all different kinds of sad stories there. I had a small diamond ring that I left on the top of the toilet. It was stolen within a day. I was devastated at first, then angry. I can count on my hand the times that I have lost it. That was one of them. I screamed out my frustration at one of the girls. Then it was over and done with.

One day, I was riding the subway and had a moment of clarity. *'What am I doing with my life and what am I doing here?'* I had tears in my eyes and thought about going home with my tail between my legs. What would everyone think of me? More importantly, what would my mom and dad say?

I did fly home eventually. I vividly remember sitting on my bedroom floor against the wall crying. My dad came in and sat beside me. I said, "Dad, I am so ashamed of what I have done."

He paused and replied, "There are things I am not so proud of, too." Thank God for understanding and compassionate people like my dad.

Even though I was never pushed or counselled to go to University, I knew that I had to. I thought about being a physiotherapist, so I enrolled in science courses at the University of Regina. I took anatomy, psychology, and calculus. Our psychology teacher was completely off the wall. I found out later that he was involved in extensive psychotropic drug testing. I learned a great deal in my anatomy class, but we dissected cats. They were scrawny, hairless, and smelled like formaldehyde. For exams, we had to identify the different organs and muscle groups. I thought, "I am learning a lot, but this is disgusting." Calculus was a complete waste of my time.

In year two, I made a complete one-eighty and switched to drama. I took ballet, acting, scenic and costume design, plus dramatic history. I loved most of the classes. Our ballet instructor was Reg Hawe and he barked at us with a cigarette hanging out of his mouth. He would also stand up once in a while with his big potbelly to demonstrate. I wore pink tights, leotard, and ballet slippers. The men in our classes were ninety percent gay and always entertaining, not unlike figure skaters.

For the first two years of university, I lived with my sister Charlotte. We got along for the most part, but she was somewhat puzzled by my sporadically, energized behaviour. You could say that I went through a promiscuous few years. I discovered sex at the ripe age of nineteen and thought I could wield my power over men. I had many a lover and only one or two boyfriends during my first three years at University. I didn't really have time for them. I had two jobs teaching skating and waitressing plus a full course load.

Like many women at my age and in the eighties, I went on the pill. Within a short time, I had developed endometriosis. One night, it was so painful that Charlotte had to take me to emergency. They gave me a heavy dose of painkillers. Eventually, I had a surgery called a D & C—dilation and curettage—to remove tissue from inside my uterus. My doctor told me that I had so much excess blood that, "An ectopic pregnancy cannot be ruled out." He also said, "Go about your regular activities." A day after my surgery, I went for a ten-kilometre run. Afterwards, I had bad cramps and once again had to rely on painkillers. I went off the pill and never saw that doctor again.

Regina, Saskatchewan may be a small city of one hundred thousand, but it had plenty of arts and culture. The folk festival in the summer was quite an attraction and of course, there was the Center of the Arts. My dramoid friends and I had two main hangouts—The Owl, which was the University bar, and Formerly pub in the Hotel Saskatchewan. We danced to some great bands at the University and had plenty of drinks in the gay, quirky character destination tucked away as a hotel afterthought.

I have lifelong friends from my time at the University of Regina. Most of them lived in the same old brick apartment building three blocks from the drama department. I had my own bachelor suite that I loved. It had hardwood floors and huge windows with big poplar trees outside. The block was a frequent hang out for male prostitution. It was fun to watch the drama unfolding right outside my window.

My best friends were Amelia, Lisa, and David. Amelia and Lisa were both feisty, headstrong, and temperamental. Amelia had a signature two-inch scar under her lip and Lisa was as photogenic as a model. However, she was dishevelled most of the time and her apartment in the lower level was a complete mess. David was a closet gay fellow who was, back then, quiet, sensitive, and very good-looking with the most amazing light blue eyes. At one point, we all lived in the same two-storey old house three blocks from the University drama department. I had a suite on the main floor, and they had the larger one on the second floor. It was communal living at its best in the eighties. Artists love hanging out with other artists.

David and Lisa dated for a short time; however, David may have had a little crush on my cousin Rob.

There was a love triangle between me, a temporary boyfriend, David, and Lisa. Lisa slept with my boyfriend, I slept with David — although it was quite harmless and funny, and Rob was on the sidelines probably patiently waiting for David to come to his senses. What is it like to know that you are gay and still be attracted to a woman's energy? Lisa was furious with David and me, but how could she be when she'd had a wee fling with my boyfriend? Was she jealous of our friendship? I wonder how Amelia felt about the whole scenario. The bottom line was we were all exceptionally good friends and would be for an exceedingly long time.

David and I were kindred spirits with a shared love of nature, art, gardening, design, food, and entertaining. We went on a canoeing/camping weekend down the South Saskatchewan River which was extraordinary. We pulled the canoe and supplies on soft white sand in clear, sparkling river water for miles. We camped on scarcely treed islands, cooking over a fire and watching deer, birds, and any other creatures we could spot. We were like children playing in the field of nature. Our love for adventure continued when he eventually moved to Vancouver, British Columbia and then Victoria on Vancouver Island. There is so much beauty in the world — especially in a country called Canada.

Explore the World

Never lose your childlike curiosity for the world.

I completed my drama degree in 1987. Now what? It was time to travel and see the world. My best friend Amelia and I signed up for the Student Work Abroad Program. We were to live and work in London, England. We had a stopover in Toronto that turned into an eight-hour delay. We drank Black Russians in an airport bar. I was loaded and stumbled onto the plane. I was ghostly white for most of the trip. We arrived in London in the wee hours of the morning. To the SWAP office, we went for our orientation. We ended up living in a large house in Cricklewood with a bunch of Canadians. I worked at Harrods in the retail food department. That lasted for barely three months. I was fired because I didn't show up for work a few times. We were in London for a couple of disasters. One was the King's Cross fire that wreaked havoc in the subway system. The other was a windstorm that uprooted trees and shut the city down for a day or two. We were safe.

It was time to leave London and use our Eurorail passes. Our goal was to travel by train to the hottest destination in Europe we could find. How about Crete, Greece? So, south we went. We travelled through France and Italy with no time to stop. We had a destination in mind. We were in Brindisi, Italy and waited for the next ferry to the island of Greece. I was sick as a dog for most of the trip. I had some sort of bug. Back then, there were no computers or Blackberrys so we pretty much flew by the seat of our pants and hoped for the best. We made our way to the southernmost tip of Greece and figured out that we needed to get to a port town to take another ferry to Crete. We hired a taxi driver who took us on curvy up-and-down roads to a sleepy little spot on the map. From there, we had an eight-hour ferry ride to the lovely island of Crete.

I remember arriving in the morning and seeing a town built on a hill. I could smell the salty sea air and I could hear the sweet silence of the island. I saw white and red clay roofs sparkling in the sun. We had made it. It was December. Now, we needed a place to live. We followed an old lady on a goat up a hill. I am not sure why, but then we went back down the hill and ended up hanging out with a British guy on the beach. We found a cheap hotel near the beach with the lovely sights, sounds, and smell of the ocean. We lived on bread, feta cheese, and tomatoes. I fell asleep to the lull of the waves on the shore.

I remember being on a cliff looking west towards the ocean. Canada and my home, so far, yet so close. I could almost touch it. It was almost time to go back and experience winter. But, not yet. Not yet.

We stayed on the island of Crete for a couple of weeks and then made our way back to Athens. We stayed at a youth hostel and celebrated Christmas there. Athens is a beautiful, historic city with many sites to see. I wandered around parks and kept running into thousands of years of history. My friend and I thought perhaps we should make some money. So, we tried out olive picking. It had rained earlier so we had to be careful on the slippery, wet trees. We did not have a clue about what we were doing. We were fired on the spot.

From Athens, we hopped on a train to Istanbul. It was an old uncomfortable train that made its way across the Greek and Turkish border in the middle of the night. We stopped and looked out the window. There were men with guns. Cooperatively, we disembarked the train and showed our passports. We were there for a few hours. We arrived in Istanbul the next day just in time for New Years'. Much to our chagrin, we discovered that Turkey did not celebrate New Year's. Unceremoniously, we had drinks in a quiet bar.

Istanbul was a fascinating city with a mosque

on every street corner. We went to the big covered market called the Grand Bazaar and had tea with the merchants. It was a way to lure tourists and then make the sale. The tea was good. They were passionate but they did not persuade. At night, we were harassed by men. Amelia was blond so she got the brunt of it. They were even so bold as to grab her ass. She barked back at them like a crazy American. It didn't seem to work.

We brought Turkish bread into our sparse room only to discover that, in the morning, mice had been at it. Live and learn. We thought it would be a good idea to have a Turkish bath for cheap. We were held in the arms of a plump Turkish woman who scrubbed and bathed us in warm water. She even shaved our legs for us! We deserved that little luxury. At the train station, we found some telephones so we thought it would be a good idea to call home. My mom and dad could not believe we were in Istanbul. They warned us to be careful. We met a nice Austrian fellow on the train back to the ferry. He invited us to visit him and his family in Austria. We would consider it.

We were back in Italy and it was time to explore the beautiful country. One city after another: Rome, Florence, Venice, Milan; a day or two in each. Each had its own special appeal. I loved Rome for its history; Florence for its gardens and beauty; Venice for its romantic waterways and bridges. I will go back. Milan was not my favourite. It was a big, dirty, sprawling city. It was grey and cold for that time of year.

In mid-January, we decided to reconnect with Charlie in Austria. He lived with his parents in a village not far from Innsbruck. We arrived and were immediately taken care of by his parents with a traditional Austrian lunch of cured meats and bread. They still had their Christmas tree up with candles and all. Was that not a fire hazard?

Recreational activities were very important to Charlie. Austrians get at least two months paid holiday so they make good use of their time off. He took us hang-gliding and skiing in Innsbruck. We skied down the mountain where *James Bond* had been filmed. We ended the day with mulled wine in the ski village. I felt like I was living the true European winter lifestyle.

Charlie invited us to southern France so off we went by car to the ocean. It was still winter, of course, but we had a picnic on the beach. We ended up staying in a two-hundred-year-old stone cottage. It was nestled in the trees covered in moss. It was sweet and cozy. My friend and Charlie had hooked up, so to speak. I was happy to be on my own. It is good to be with oneself. I have more confidence, awareness, and focus. The world unfolds in all of its splendour for the eyes to see. We spent the weekend in St. Tropez. The weather was mild for that time of year. Or, maybe it just seemed to be since we are from Canada. In our cottage, we drank gallons of wine and ate like kings. We made fires in the old stone fireplace and roasted shishkabobs. I thought to myself, "Can these lovely, leisurely days last?" No, because it was time to travel to the next country: Spain.

You may think that this is beginning to sound like a travelogue. It is not. We spent a week in Spain. "The rain in Spain falls mainly on the plain." Our first stop was Madrid. It was rainy and dreary. It is a big, sprawling city with a McDonald's every three blocks. So, off we went south to Barcelona. On our way, we stopped in Toledo, a beautiful walled city. We hung out there for a day and drank beer with some American students. Then, we took a night train to Seville. The weather was beautiful and we spent most of our time sunning ourselves on a dock by the river. We ate tapas, drank wine, and generally had a pleasant time. The Spanish people are friendly, animated, and accommodating. We would buy lunch at small shops and the owners would be happy and very interested in who we were and what we were doing in Spain. Next stop: Barcelona. I loved that city. I was particularly impressed with the Picasso museum. It was a lovely home in a courtyard that showed many works from throughout his entire career. Barcelona, like many European cities, is a beautiful walking place. So, we walked for miles along skinny, stone streets and admired the sites. The unfinished Gaudi cathedral was spectacular. He was ahead of his time.

We made our way to the coast to Lisboa. I thought the Spanish people were kind and then I met the Portuguese. On the train, we met an incredibly nice lady who offered us an apartment at a good price. We shared this wonderful place with a couple of swell fellows from England. We hung out like a little family. I was not alone. I hooked up with one of the friendly British fellows who was quite fond of me. We had non-stop sex for several days. Oh, how wonderfully free we can be in our twenties.

On the weekend, we headed six hours south to Lagos. We spent time on the beach and generally just enjoyed the lazy days on the coast of Portugal.

Sadly, our European adventure was coming to an end. You see, we were running out of money and time. We took night trains through Seville, Madrid, and Paris. It is quite amazing to fall asleep on a train and wake up in another country. We made our way back to London where it all began. We flew out of London back to Canada and home. It was good to be home. Recently, my dad said, "I took out a life insurance policy on you when you went to Europe with Amelia." Perhaps that was a good idea at the time.

Go East then West

Live life spherically – in all directions

Back in Regina, I met a quirky, drunk fellow at the University bar one night. He brazenly came up to me and asked, "Will you marry me?" Funny enough, I realized that it had been my only marriage proposal to date. His name was Steve Taylor and I guess if I had married him, I would have been Elizabeth Taylor. I thought he was nuts but his loss of inhibition, drunk or not, intrigued me. We had a drink together with Amelia and he blabbed on about god knows what. We exchanged phone numbers and that was that.

He pursued me relentlessly for the whole summer of 1998. He bought me flowers all the time, took me out to live music venues, and entertained me with his insanely, off the wall sense of humour. I was working at Celebrations Dinner Theater at the time and he came to a few of our after-production parties. All my dramoid friends liked him because not only was he amusing, but he treated me like gold.

We had an instant sexual attraction. It was a summer romance that was filled with sex, parties, swimming at the outdoor Wascana park pool, going to the folk festival and enjoying being twenty-five and carefree. Summer days in Regina were long, hot, and sultry. I lived with Charlotte in a 1940s post-war house with sweltering bedrooms on the second floor. Steve and I had long sex sessions in the cool basement bedroom, trying not to disturb my sister. I am certain she had an inkling of what was going on. However, she was busy working as an executive assistant at the Saskatchewan Wheat Pool in downtown Regina.

Steve worked at a convenience store, sometimes late into the evening. He always called me when he was finished, and we made plans to meet. I don't remember sleeping very much that summer. I was busy at the dinner theatre, playing all kinds of characters, including a precocious French girl named Fifi and an annoying, nutty granny character in our Country Show. We stayed in character for a full three hours on and off stage as we not only acted, sang, and danced, but we served, too. It was super fun and hilarious to improv our way at tables as crazy characters. One night, we finished the show with a song and were all lined up at the front of the stage. We were moving forward with the music and then the stage started moving forward towards the audience. I spontaneously said, "Oh my god, the stage is moving!" right into the microphone. My co-actor Garth still relives that story. The cast was mainly University of Regina drama graduates, weirdly talented and hilarious. The shows were physically demanding but who could feel that at the age of twenty-six? I was also in love and that alone has boundless energy.

My best friend Amelia moved to Toronto that summer and I was inclined to follow her. I wanted to study dance at York University. Steve didn't take the news so well, but he did surprise me by showing up at the train station to send me off. He ran up to the platform in a Bugs Bunny sweatshirt and we stood on the platform and kissed goodbye. It was like a scene from a film. He didn't run on the platform like the Beatles in a *Hard Day's Night* or Owen Wilson, Adrien Brody, and Jason Schwartzman in *The Darjeeling Limited*. I, however, stood on the train door stair as it pulled away from the station and yelled, "I love you, Steve Taylor!" I heard him reply with a grin on his face, "You bitch." Perhaps he should have run from the train station.

It was one of the last trains to go from Regina through Manitoba and Ontario. It had a skylight and a bar car. I watched a wicked lightning show through the Saskatchewan prairies while listening to the Proclaimers' *I'm Gonna Be (500 miles)* on my Walkman. I stared out the window and daydreamed about my new life. One night in the bar car, I hung out with a group of people and did mushrooms (the magic kind). I was a little high for most of the night and fell in love with a green-eyed girl sitting beside me. If I were a lesbian, she could have been my girlfriend.

I didn't stop in Toronto. I kept going to Montreal. My destination was Halifax and Sydney, Nova Scotia as I had some Celebration Dinner Theater actor friends there. I fell in love with Montreal as soon as I stepped off the train. Who wouldn't love a French walking city in summer? I met my friend Lisa's boyfriend there, who was my tour guide. Combine "old-world European charm" with a vibrant North American city and voila, Montreal. I loved the outdoor sidewalk cafes, late night clubs, and walking in old Montreal founded in 1642. No time for Cirque du Soleil or the Montreal Canadians hockey league because off I went, back on the train to the Maritimes. The trains in Eastern Canada were modern and fast. I approached the city of Halifax in less than twenty-four hours.

I met my wild and crazy friend Rosalie there and we immediately hit Grafton Street where all the bars were. The pubs were very much a University scene, so we went to the infamous Lower Deck, founded in 1887 and situated beautifully on Upper Water Street. It had long, old wooden tables where everyone congregated to eat fish and chips, drink beer, and listen to live music. Maritimers, being from the motherlands of Ireland and

Scotland, are super friendly and fun.

I spent a couple of days wandering around Halifax and then got back on the train to Sydney on Cape Breton Island, where my fiery redheaded girlfriend Kelly lived. She affectionately called it, "the ass-hole of the earth," as it is the most Eastern end of Canada. I love lighthouses and there were a few there. I love the ocean and there is one there too with rocky shores and dreamy beaches. My friend drove me along the famous Cabot Trail. It was named after Italian explorer John Cabot (Giovanni Caboto) who arrived in 1497, sailing under control by King Henry VII of England. Cabot met the Mi'kmaq people who were the native folk of Cape Breton Island.

It was the end of summer, so the undulating Cabot Trail was not on fire yet—as in the trees. In the fall, the maples turn all shades of red, orange, and yellow. I love Eastern Canada for many reasons, but the Cabot Trail is a must-see for the sunset views, trees, and the untouched Eastern coastline.

I made my way back to Toronto as I was beginning university in September and started teaching figure skating for the York Figure Skating Club. I stayed with Amelia for a short time. Steve wrote to me almost every day with long, hilarious, and heartfelt letters. To this day, I have never been pursued like that. Do men even write handwritten letters anymore? He was living and working in Kananaskis, Alberta, one hour from Calgary at the ski resort. He called it "Can an ass kiss." We missed each other terribly but I was too busy and focused to worry about it. That attitude probably made him chase me even more.

I loved my dance classes at York. I took ballet, modern, dance history, and music. I rode the subway every day from school to several rinks and home. I found a lovely Asian fellow to share a house with. It was near Dundas West station. I remember a "doughnut shop" on the corner. I went in to get some pastries only to discover there were none. I think it was a drug dealer hangout.

By November, we, Steve and I both, caved and he booked a flight to Toronto. I was so excited; I could barely contain myself. He landed early in the morning, so I decided to wear my pyjamas, ride the airport bus, and surprise him. We made out at the back of the bus and continued to do so for three days straight, only to break for meals and the occasional walk in High Park. We were in love and on a non-stop course to eventually living together. We said our goodbyes at the airport, and I must have looked forlorn because an older lady said, "Don't worry, he'll be back."

After Christmas, just five months after we met, he moved to Toronto. We rented a suite in a three-storey old house in the beautiful High Park area, once again near the subway station. Steve found a job as a teller at a bank and I continued to not only teach skating and go to school but worked as a waitress part-time, too.

The first year was blissful. We played house as I cooked, and he cleaned in between our mercenary duties and happy hours. Every Sunday morning, we watched *Coronation Street*, read the newspaper, and relaxed. We drank virgin Caesars, rum and cokes, beer, and wine. We hosted BBQs and dinner parties. One-time, Steve put on his rollerblades and performed a figure-skating-like routine in the back alley. We all laughed our heads off. We befriended a couple on the main floor of our house named Janine and Dwayne. Janine was Australian and Dwayne was Canadian. She was a hoot and loved Canadian alcoholic beverages, food, and friendly, down to earth fun. She wore a red and black lumberjack shirt and drank Canadian beer as an homage to our land.

Steve joined an English soccer league and I would hang out on the sidelines, proudly watching him. After the game, we would go to the pub and obnoxiously drink and party with his soccer buddies. It was the 1990 World Cup Soccer summer hosted by Italy with Uruguay and Italy as a highlight game and Germany versus Argentina in the final. Toronto had a huge Italian community and the city was abuzz with parties and soccer hysteria. The energy of the city was contagious. We joined in on the mayhem with non-stop parties and horn honking. By the way, Germany won and the whole event was described as "Every match was like a final."

In the fall and winter, I was stressed out by my non-stop schedule. University was a huge commitment and so were the demands of being a professional figure skating coach. I quit the waitressing job as my boss was an asshole. Steve was stressed at the bank because his boss was an idiot, too. We were both twenty-six years of age, away from our families, and living in a city of over three million people. I had wicked mood swings and crying fits of frustration and even anger. Steve shut down emotionally, as men often do. That made matters worse. One time, I threw a glass of water on him to get his attention. He said next to nothing. I stormed off in a huff and stayed the night at a girlfriend's place. The next day, I returned, hoping that he would talk to me, but he just sat in the backyard, drank rum, and read the newspaper.

We were slowly and painfully growing apart. For my birthday in May, Steve bought me a fondue set. I laughed after opening it, thinking it was a joke. He was devastated and said, "I thought we could cut up meat and fruit and have a picnic." I was horrified at my behaviour and to this day, I never balk at receiving gifts of any kind. I flew home to Saskatchewan for a break.

I thought that distance would give us perspective. I came back to Toronto only to find out that things were not going to change.

In the summer of 1991, Steve went back to Regina and then to Calgary, Alberta. I went back to Regina and stayed with my sister Charlotte for the summer. I was devastated and spent the summer in mourning and found odd jobs to do, including a short stint at Red Lobster.

Calgary seemed like a logical choice for places to live. It was a bigger city, a nine-hour drive from Radville, and had opportunities. In the back of my mind, I thought there was a possibility of Steve and I reuniting. I packed up my car with all my belongings and said good-bye to my sister. I said, "There is a huge part of me that wants to stay, and the same part of me that needs to go." I needed to be courageous.

It was a long drive from Regina to Calgary across the prairie, lost in my thoughts. My car broke down in Brooks, two hours east of Calgary. I was delayed a few hours waiting for the shop to fix it. I was exhausted when I finally arrived. The only people I knew were Steve, who was not speaking to me, and my cousin Rob. I lived in a one-bedroom apartment in Bankview. I turned on the stove hood fan to comfort me at night. I was starting over again in a new city and I was scared and lonely. The feeling wasn't new to me. Once again,

I looked long and hard at my situation and decided that I had only one choice: make the best of it.

It was fall and I had a job teaching figure skating in Springbank, twenty kilometres west of Calgary. My colleague's name was Joy and she was a delight to work with. We carpooled every morning and then again later in the afternoon. My schedule looked like my amateur skating days. Joy and I met Geoff, who partnered dance at the club. He had a beautiful condo west of Calgary and invited us for happy hour drinks nearly every Friday after skating. Geoff and I immediately bonded and became inseparable friends. My ex-boyfriend faded from my memory.

Springbank Hill, in the district of Rockyview, is a beautiful area overlooking the Rocky Mountain foothills. It is rich with cattle farming and mansions on acreages. Calgary was enjoying an oil boom in the early nineties and rich folk flocked to Springbank. The skating students were awesome but some of the parents were a pain in the ass. Hockey and figure skating parents can be that way. I made good money and enrolled in dance courses at the University of Calgary. I loved my modern dance classes because the teachers were crazy creative. They also gave me a chance to express my self through dance since I was no longer skating solo.

Soon, I made plenty of friends, gay and straight

alike. Geoff and I both hosted plenty of themed dinner parties: martinis, cocktails, gourmet food, hired young, good-looking bartenders, Halloween, Christmas, Calgary Stampede, and everything in between. My cousin Rob and I became good friends again and he and I hosted yearly Academy Awards parties. A few times, he booked a room at the Westin Hotel, rented a big screen TV, ordered appetizers, and everyone dressed up to the nines. My parties involved smart cocktails, gourmet food, ballads, and prizes.

I moved from my small apartment in Bankview to a large two-bedroom condo in the same area. From there, I rented another two-bedroom westward in Killarney, complete with a deck and backyard area. One summer day, I rented a hot tub that was delivered, filled, and ready for a party. The guests were gay with a few straight men thrown in just to balance out the evening. We were so loud and obnoxious the cops came and told us to shut it down. As they were leaving, they did ask, "Hey, where did you get that hot tub?"

I eventually saved enough money from teaching and waitressing to buy my first condo in Bankview. I paid for half of the downpayment and Dad generously paid for the other half. This condo was a labour of love. It was gutted and restored with hardwood floors and new stainless-steel appliances. I painted the main floor walls a calming sage green and my upstairs bedroom a rich Merlot. I had my favourite prints on the walls and a cute balcony covered with flowers. My mom and dad visited a few times and she said, "This home is almost too sensual." I considered that a compliment.

I had many a lover but no boyfriends. My gay friends were my boyfriends. Natalie was my best girlfriend at the time and recently she said, "We are lucky to be alive." She was a nutty yet super-talented art and design graduate from the Alberta College of Art and Design. We planned rafting trips down the Elbow River near her apartment and got caught in many hailstorms. There were always alcoholic beverages to keep us warm. We dressed up as "Booze Fairies" for a Halloween party at the old Uptown Theater. We mixed all kinds of cocktails and I threw up in the cab on our way home. I continued to throw up all night with a bucket beside the couch in Natalie's apartment. She was worried I had alcohol poisoning so she called the pharmacy and they recommended anal Gravol which we called "up the bum Gravol." It worked but I was hungover for two days. At another Halloween party, Natalie showed up as Magda, the crazy leather-skinned lady from the movie *Something About Mary*. Natalie even constructed the little dog in a full white body cast. She was bang on hilarious.

Nearly a decade went by quickly as I continued to teach skating, dance, part-time waitress and catering gigs, and exploring the famous Rocky Mountains where world-renowned places like Banff and the breathtaking Lake Louise made the scene. I joined the Alpine Club of Canada and planned yearly trips to huts and cabins perched up to ten thousand meters high in the mountains.

    A keen group of hiker friends and I ventured to these rustic huts, backpacking up gourmet food, wine, port — the important stuff — as the huts provided everything else. Faye Hut with its "Loo with a view" was my favourite, followed closely by Abbot Pass Hut overlooking Lake Louise. It was a stone cabin built in 1922 by Swiss guides in honour of Philip Stanley Abbot, who became the first mountaineering fatality in North America. Near the cabin was a pass called the Deathtrap because of its exposure to avalanches and crevasses. We stayed away from that. At night, I ventured out of the hut and onto a rock ledge to view the stars. I could almost touch them. I felt tiny like a pebble yet huge like a boulder. My heart felt like it was going to burst as I realized that there was something out there in the cosmos bigger than me and orchestrating our earthly endeavours.

    In 1994, my sister Charlotte lost her job at the Saskatchewan Wheat Pool and moved to Calgary. I was delighted to have a family member other than my cousin living close by. She had a severance package and spent three months hanging out and spending money on god knows what. She is one of the funniest people I have ever known with her self-deprecating dry sense of humour. She got along with all my friends. However, I sensed that she was lonely and made it my mission to find her someone to date. Somehow, I worked my magic with the power of intention and superb timing. My girlfriend Lynn and I met a few maritime fellas at a downtown pub. A quiet, smart younger guy intrigued me. I went home to Radville for a few days and told Lynn to set Charlotte up with Paul, come hell or high water. She did and they immediately bonded. He is ten years her junior and they have been together ever since. I was not only happy for her, but proud of my infamous matchmaking power.

In 1994, I was itching to skate again, on my own terms. I found a group of adult figure skaters that wanted to play on the ice, too. We met every Thursday night at the Glencoe Club to skate and go for drinks afterwards. We had a motley crew of twenty and thirty-somethings with a bundle of talent and desire. We formed the Calgary Professional Ice Theater and performed in Banff at a New Year's Eve celebration; Jasper for the Closing Ceremonies of the Canada Winter Games and at the Olympic Plaza in downtown Calgary skating in minus thirty degrees for a Valentine's Day Celebration. We entered the first Big

Rock Beer Commercial Contest and won! We skated to classical music with beers in our hands. It was a clever and undoubtedly memorable experience filming it and receiving our award of three thousand dollars (split amongst the group), and Big Rock T-shirts and beer mugs.

I practiced at the Olympic Oval at the University nearly every day at noon. There were few skaters there and the ice was superlative. I played and skated to all kinds of inspiring music. I choreographed two programs called "The Opera" and "Sugar in My Bowl" by Nina Simone. Geoff made me a beautifully flowing skating outfit and said, "Lizzie, I have never seen you so happy." It was the happiest time for me as a skater. I learned the art of performing and I had a group of skating friends for support. I was not alone.

Our last performance was in Strathmore, a small city east of Calgary. It was called The Art of the Edge. Mom and Dad travelled to Calgary to attend, along with my oldest brother Allen and Nephew Andrew. I had two solos and performed them eloquently with ease and love for my family. I felt like I was floating across the ice. At the end of the program, my nephew Andrew gave me a red rose by the boards. My heart soared. Mom said afterwards, "You didn't tell us you were the star of the show." I didn't feel like I was a "star" but maybe to them, I was.

Daisy Duck

Manifest your vision and dreams
Watch them unfold
Become Anthropomorphic

My good friend Linda from the Ice Theater joined Disney on Ice and was touring the Philippines. I confess that I was the green-eyed monster — envious. I had the travel bug and was itching to go somewhere far away and vastly different from Calgary. I was thirty-five years old, in my sixteenth year of teaching skating, and frustrated with being alone especially during the long winters. Linda told me that the next tour was the United States and Australia. I thought, *'This is perfect! Time to seize an opportunity.'*

I put together an audition tape, letter to the casting director, sent it off to the States, and hoped for the best. Two months later, during the Christmas holidays, I found out that I was cast in the show. I was elated. I had only two weeks to prepare and pack. I bought a huge rolling suitcase that was the size of a small refrigerator. What the hell does one take on tour in the States for ten weeks? I left it open for a few days, hoping that I could narrow it down to essential things like skates, clothes for all weather, photo album, and journal. My cat Puddy ("Poodzy"), a huge tabby cat, hung out in the case and was no help at all. My sister Charlotte, however, was helpful as she was going to live in my condo and look after the cat while I was touring.

I left on a cold early morning in January. I dragged my heavy suitcase down the stairs while Puddy ran after me. He was whinging and I was heartbroken. I kept hauling him up the stairs and he kept running down. It was like a scene from *Lassie Go Home*. Finally, I put him upstairs in my bedroom. The cab was waiting, and I was on a new adventure.

I flew to Atlanta, Georgia and was bused out to Rome for two weeks of rehearsal. It was on the bus that I decided to change my name to "Lizzie." Charlotte and I adored *Pride and Prejudice* with Elizabeth and Jane Bennet. Jane would say, "Oh, Lizzie," and I thought, *'Yes, I am a Lizzie, not a Liz. But, I'll always be Elizabeth to my parents.'*

I spontaneously called my ex-boyfriend Lee in Atlanta. He was completely flabbergasted to hear from me. He was in his office and we chatted about the show and his married life with a new child. We ended up having hot phone sex. Men are so easy. I had no time to waste because rehearsals started immediately.

I was excited and nervous as I didn't know anyone except Linda and I had to learn five new routines, including my claim to fame as Daisy Duck. Our director, Greg, was kind and good at what he did. My fellow cast members were from all over the world. Ninety percent of them were younger than me, slightly immature, and had high strung figure skater egos. The Russians were snobs, the Americans were high on themselves, and the Canadians (with a couple of Australians thrown in) were down to earth and super friendly.

We lived in cheap hotel rooms and I soon figured out that our salaries sucked. I guess that's why Disney and Feld Entertainment are stinking rich. Going out for food all the time was completely out of the question. I purchased a hot plate and pot and lived on noodles. It was like being at university. In between the long days of rehearsal, we had costume fittings and press briefings. I soon learned the lay of the land.

We toured through cities like Columbus, Ohio and Little Rock, Arkansas. Some weeks, we would do three shows per day, finish at nine in the evening and hop onto an all-night bus ride to god knows where next. For the few days we got off, I explored the city and shopped for cheap groceries. My favourite cities were southern like Mobile, Lafayette (we called "laugh me up"), and Baton Rouge. Baton Rouge had a rich musical history, but I ended up going to gay bars with the fun gay boys on tour. Curtis was Canadian, hot, and had a great sense of humour. We went to a bar and ended up playing pool. There was a lesbian there who seemed to take a liking to me. We played pool, danced, and hung out and drank cocktails. At the end of the evening, I said, "Got to call it a night." The girl piped up and said, "Don't go yet, all I want to do is buy you a steak and a beer!" Curtis laughed his head off and to this day has never let me live it down on Facebook. That was the best offer I had on tour.

I was fascinated by the history of the south. I toured plantation houses like Nottaway, right next to the Mississippi River, that blew my mind. It is the largest antebellum Greek revival, Italianate-styled mansion in the South built in 1859 by John Randolph. He turned the cotton fields to sugar cane, owned one hundred and seventy-six enslaved people, making him one of the larger slaveholders in the South. I saw the slave quarters and tried to imagine what life had been like for them. I tried to forget that horrific time in American history by the sheer wonder of the immensity of the house with its virginal white room (now hosting weddings), the ornate gold room, and emerald green music room.

Our technical crew was led by a couple of twenty-something guys from Texas. They referred to African

American folk as "niggers." I was shocked and appalled. I am not saying that Canada is perfect by any means, but I had never in my life heard that word in person—only at the movies and in television series and like *Roots*. I believed and still believe in being inclusive, not exclusive and racism in any form is not cool.

For a break from the gruelling tour, a few of us went to *Pocahontas* (which we jokingly called "poke your haunches") in Chicago. I walked the Magnificent Mile, checking out art galleries, shops, and eating some great food. The show was all right but not as good as our Disney classics variety show. Pocahontas, a native American ten-year-old had a tough go of it. In Disneyland and on ice, not so much.

Being Daisy Duck had its challenges. The costume was hot, and I wore a headband to keep my hair and sweat off the duck head. One time, in the middle of our routine at the beginning of the show, my headband fell over my eyes. I couldn't see much except a few dark images of swirling skaters around me. Daisy was in a panic, blindly looking for the outline of the Castle backdrop. I miraculously fumbled my way there as the backstage dudes yelled, "What's wrong?"

"I can't see!" An arm yanked me through the curtain, and I stumbled onto the carpet runner. Daisy was saved. Another time, I had to fill in as the driver of Cinderella's carriage. There was a steering wheel, reigns, and a power pedal. The coach was all lit up and it was led by a team of big boys in horse costumes. It glittered and glowed as the horses pranced ahead of the coach. I dropped the reigns accidentally and the horses pranced way ahead of the carriage. I put the pedal to the metal, trying to catch up to them. The ice had a slick layer of water on it and the carriage started to spin around the corner. Being a good Saskatchewan driver on ice, I handled the wheel like a real pro, avoiding a complete three hundred and sixty-degree turn with poor Cinderella being spun around. All was well as Cinderella waved to the crowd like the Queen of England. She and the prince lived happily and ever after.

The tour ended in Lafayette, Louisiana, April 1998. I was exhausted and relieved to not only leave the gruelling tour but to take a break from the group of obnoxious skaters. One of the managers needed a rental car taken back to a small town not far from New Orleans. I gladly offered to drive it as I made my way along Highway 90, blasting tunes and feeling free as a bird. It reminded me of my first car — a bright, lime green 1976 Plymouth Valiant. It was kind of a piece of junk but at the time, not to me. It was the freedom to drive alone on the thirty miles to Weyburn at the age of eighteen.

I spent a couple of days alone in New Orleans before meeting my friend Geoff and his boyfriend Wade. I loved roaming around the French Quarter, taking the Saint Charles and Desire streetcars through all kinds of fascinating neighbourhoods and taking a stroll around spooky Anne Rice's house. New Orleans was more intoxicating at night with the sounds of jazz and blues and the spicy smells of creole cuisine. I got hooked on po' boy sandwiches with breaded oysters the size of the palm of your hand. Late in the evening, a strange fog drifted in from the Mississippi River, giving the city a haunted, eerie ambiance. I found it mesmerizing.

For a late-night treat, I went to Café du Monde for delightful beignets and café au lait. I felt a strange sense of home, feeling the familiarity of Saskatchewan and Louisiana. I saw the vast plains of Louisiana and the long, sultry sunsets. I felt my homeland of the prairies and a sense of freedom as well. Isn't America the land of the free?

Geoff and Wade joined me in New Orleans, and we stayed in a flat a few blocks away from the main street in the French Quarter. It was April and thank god we had missed Mardi Gras. The city was abuzz and busy enough without all of the tomfooleries. Geoff and I hung out at a gay strip bar until the wee hours. By two in the morning, I thought it was time to go back to the flat. Geoff was drunk and busy tucking several dollar bills into the underwear of the young male strippers on the bar. I tempted fate by walking in the middle of the night alone a few blocks in one of the most dangerous cities in the United States. I made it to the door of the flat but was followed by a big black man. Wade was inside the flat sleeping and I was locked out. I banged on the door and yelled, "Open the door, let me in!" The big black man approached the steps and shamelessly placed his hand on my bottom. I cried out, "How dare you!" Thankfully, Wade opened the door just in the nick of time. I must have had a guardian angel that night.

After saying goodbye to my friends, I hopped on the Amtrak train from New Orleans to Los Angeles. I loved the train, even the old one that went clickety-clack across the plains of Louisiana, Texas, and finally through southern California. I went through four states in less than four days. My destination was Las Vegas, Nevada. I visited my old skating buddy from Weyburn, Saskatchewan. I was more interested in seeing David than I was in touring Las Vegas. He was happy to see me, too, and he and his partner showed me a few of the sights, including Siegfried & Roy. The Siberian white tigers were cool, but S & R freaked me out. Apparently, Roy was freaked out by a tiger, too. Perhaps Americans should stay away from tigers, the same way that Canadians should stay clear of bears.

I was thrilled when I made it back to Calgary. It was awesome to see my cat again and not live out of a suitcase. I cooked, cleaned, and enjoyed the comforts of home. It was spring and time for a birthday. I had a reunion with my friends and Charlotte had a Daisy Duck cake made. Perhaps my claim to fame as Daisy was true after all. A month flew by and then it was time to prepare for a journey to the land down under.

Australia was big and beautiful in so many ways. Interestingly enough, my favourite was not the ocean or the beaches but the desert. In a way, it reminded me of the prairies. It is an ocean of earthly colours like yellow, brown, green, orange, and red with clean sand, rock formations, and canyons that pop in and out of the land.

Disney's first destination was Perth, Western Australia. Once again, the skating tour got thrown into two to three shows a day, six days a week. The difference was that instead of all-night bus rides, we flew from one major city to the next. In one way, I felt like a rockstar. In another way, I was a la-la land, overworked and underpaid Disney character. We played in Perth, Newcastle, Brisbane, Sydney, Melbourne, and ended in Adelaide, South Australia. I only had a taste of each city that involved the inside of a makeshift rink, hotels, and gay nightclubs.

It was winter down under but still warm for a Canadian. We had late night exhausting rehearsals in Perth but stayed at a swanky hotel compared to the budget hotels of America. And, there were no overnight bus trips as we flew from one city to the next. I collected a shwack load of Airmiles on that tour.

Melbourne had the funkiest nightclubs and the best after-hour parties. Sydney had the best drag shows, strip clubs, and cheap take-out food joints like "Tum Tum Thai Takeaway." I tried ecstasy in Sydney and was disappointed when the lovey-dovey feeling lasted only one hour. I walked all over Sydney on our few days off and marvelled at the Sydney Harbor Bridge and Opera House. I took ferry rides from the Quay to beaches like Bondi and Manley. Curtis, the gorgeous gay dude who tried to set me up with a lesbian in Baton Rouge, came with me one afternoon. We re-enacted the *Titanic* movie scene when Rose and Jack stood on the bow of the ship with outstretched arms... "I'm flying!" and hearing Celine Dion's *My Heart Will Go On*.

Curtis stayed up on the rail and couldn't hear the ferry driver say on the loudspeaker, "Please get down from the railing." Perhaps Rose and Jack should have got down sooner, too.

With an unexpected Disney two-thousand-dollar bonus, I changed my plane ticket and decided to port in Adelaide for a few months and tour Australia from there. I remember thinking when we received our cheques, *'Can this be right? Did they make a mistake? Do I deserve this?'* Of course, I did after being a slave worker for Disney for ten months. Ultimately, I was happy the show was over. I was physically and mentally exhausted and needed to re-group and re-charge. Crazy as it was, everyone else on tour went back home except for me and the token Australian in the show named Simon. What were they thinking? How often does a person travel twenty hours to get to the land down under?

I stayed with some friends of friends, rested, and planned my next adventure. I shared a ride with Simon who lived in Adelaide and we made our way across the fertile lands of South Australia. We camped out under the stars and I heard strange sounds like crazy monkeys. It turned out to be the cackle of a kookaburra. I was terrified at first to sleep out in the elements surrounded by wildlife but after a while realized there was nothing to fear. I rolled herself up tight in a fetal position under a manmade tarp-like tent and fell asleep to the sounds of wild Australia.

During the show, I'd had brief moments of loneliness and sadness. They would come and go like the tour buses and planes rolling in and out of countless cities. I was cognizant of it but then oblivious as my journey changed with the wind. Driving with Simon, I had trouble concentrating and making decisions. Simon finally said, "Jeez you are indecisive." I heard him but soon brushed it off as I decided to be dumped off in Byron Bay, an eastern coastal town in New South Wales.

It is a beautiful lazy community with plenty of surfers and travellers who ended up staying there for months or even years. The highrises are in Brisbane but none in sight around Byron Bay as the council has imposed height restrictions. I saw no view obstruction of north or south beaches, Captain Cook lookout with sunset views, and the Cape Byron Lighthouse which is the most easterly point of Australia mainland. I even explored inland through the rain forest and saw a stunning sight called Minyon Falls. Other than Niagara Falls in Ontario, I had not seen falls that size before. I hung out in this lazy good vibe town at the hostel and walked north and south along the beach. I even tried surfing once. The board was twice as big as me and the waves seemed to charge at me like a formidable wall that I had no chance of scaling. It was very scary and exhausting, to say the least. I cut myself on the surfboard and thought, "I have had quite enough of this."

My next stop was Arlie Beach and I decided on ocean rafting to the Whitsunday Islands. The seventy-four islands lie between the northeast coast of Queensland and the Great Barrier Reef. I was with a group that was boated out to the islands by a high-powered catamaran. I explored the famous Whitehaven Beach with its soft sand as white as snow. The water was warm and like floating in a bath. It was a remote paradise.

There was no time to waste because I was headed north to Cannes. The night before leaving, I attended a performance by the aboriginal Tjapukai dancers with the haunting sounds of the didgeridoo echoing through the warm still night. The aboriginals of Australia had it right, just like the North American natives did, until the crazy white man came along.

I went snorkelling at the Great Barrier Reef and discovered a whole other world "under the sea" just like Areole, the mermaid in the Disney show. The tour group I joined ported at Tupelo Cay, a small little white sand island about one hundred meters long. I made friends with the crew of the Passions of Paradise, the catamaran they travelled on. It had a huge motor on the back, and it hit the waves at a brisk speed like a bumpy fun ride at Disney theme parks. On the way back to Cannes, I watched the magnificent sunset over the mountains and dreamed of more adventures.

I kept travelling north as my final stop was Cape Tribulation. We travelled by bus through the Daintree rainforest and river. I saw my first baby crocodile. I loved seeing creatures in the wild—still do. Nature is perfect. Human beings, however, are far from it. I stayed at the only hostel in the rainforest called P.K.'s. I slept under a canopy of trees and listened to the creatures of the night. I took part in a rainforest walk with an interpreter named Dr. Piggy because his specialty was wild pigs. He pointed out details of the forest that a gal from Saskatchewan would not have seen if she had explored it on her own. I am talking about a sea of green with hidden little treasures of insects and powerful herbal remedies. Cape Tribulation Beach near the Daintree rainforest had small mountains, a beach, and a reef all in one place. I missed the crystal-clear box jellyfish winter season. Lucky for me because that type of Jellyfish is very potent with venom that attacks the cardiovascular system, drowning swimmers. It was a fascinating, remote place where I could lose myself in imagination and history. Walking along the remote beach, I felt a sense of doom in the pit of my stomach. I felt very much alone, isolated, and thought, "Wherever I go, there I am." The feeling passed.

  I was on a travelling mission, so I pretty much kept to myself. On my journey, I did continually meet a trio of funny, young English fellows. We drank beer together and joked about other travellers and life in general. One of them piped up and said, "Lizzie, you are one of the funniest people I know." Perhaps my sense of humour was a way of coping with my sporadic feelings of loneliness. I think that's normal for solo travellers.

I made my way to Port Douglas and hopped on the Quicksilver ferry that motored along at about fifty kilometres an hour. Back to Cannes and then I headed south to Mission Beach and decided that I needed to see the Tully River from a boat. I signed up for my first whitewater rafting trip. The river was affectionately called the "river of death." Our guide had a bandaged arm that looked not too promising. I chose to sit in the back of the raft with the guide, thinking that if I fell out, he would be able to haul me back into the boat with his one good arm. I had a blast roaring down the river with a gang of Japanese tourists who had tremendously big smiles on their faces. It was an exhilarating high of adrenaline. This was the grand finale of my eastern Australia coastal trip.

I headed south on a two-day bus ride to Victoria, New South Wales. I stayed with some lovely Australian friends of friends from Canada. I hung out for a few days with the family and I enjoyed being in a home again. I hopped on the bus again and headed back to where I had started—Adelaide, South Australia. Again, I stayed with friends and realized that it was time to get a job. I was running out of money fast. I worked at my most unique job ever in my life as a salesgirl for AAPT Smart Chat – a long-distance telephone company. I went door-to-door selling long distance packages, on rollerblades nonetheless. Having a Canadian accent and being on blades—what an easy sell! I made good cash for a few months. I made new friends in Adelaide and ended up sharing a flat with a fellow named Peter who needed a roommate for a short time.

My new adventure traveller and I packed up his old car and decided to head north to the desert. As we were packing up the car, I discovered a little friend on my shoulder. It was a big hairy Huntsman spider. I freaked out and it flew into the car somewhere. We could not find it and had to drive for a day not knowing where the creature was. It must have died because we never saw it again.

It was January and as hot as could be. Ground temperatures sometimes hit fifty degrees Celsius. We opened the windows of the car only to be bombarded by hot air like a convection oven. We stopped at a strange little town called Coober Pedy. It is so hot there, they had to build the town underground. It was a weird, little ghost town with hobbit-like inhabitants. We did not stay underground. We stayed at a cheap hotel with a cooling pool. We did explore an underground church. It was weirdly cool, quiet, and calming. Maybe all churches above or below ground are.

We left the one-horse town and went to a campsite near Kings Canyon. It was so hot we ended up sleeping outside the tent. Peter made a pass at me, but I made it clear that we were just friends. We hung out at the campsite pub and eatery. I craved a cold can of Coca-Cola. I had one with ice and to this day, that was the last can of coke I ever drank.

I adored Kings Canyon. I imagined I was in the movie *Priscilla Queen of the Desert* strutting on top of the rocks in a show gown with a tall feathered hat. We walked along the hot rocks and crevices until, low and behold, we saw an oasis. It was a cooling pool of water with trees and greenery. We immediately stripped down and went for a dip. A guide came along suddenly and suggested that we put clothes on as there was a tour group on its way.

We could not spend time in the desert without going to the famous centre of Australia called Ayers Rock, or better known as Uluru. It was two kilometres in circumference and strangely situated in the middle of the desert. Tourists spent hours watching the sunset and the spectacle of colour that transformed the rock as the minutes ticked by. There were all colours of orange, red and yellow that changed as the sun set and night approached. We got up at four in the morning to climb the rock. By six in the morning, it was almost forty degrees. Peter puked at the top. I was happy to walk around the rock and explore its different formations and regretted climbing it because the Aboriginals requested that people do not, as it was a sacred site.

Our last stop was Alice Springs. We shared an air-conditioned hotel and tried to stay cool. It was extremely hot and humid. I felt like I was going crazy. Up north, they called it the "silly season" where people do go nuts. I went on my first camel ride. They were odd, funny looking animals with bad teeth. After our two-hour ride just outside of Alice Springs, we had a traditional Australian barbecue of grilled kangaroo and ostrich. This was a fine finish to our desert adventure.

We made our way back to Adelaide safe and sound. Still no sign of the Huntsman Spider so we presumed it had died of heatstroke in the car. I extended my stay for an extra week so I could attend WOMAD—World of Music and Dance. It was spectacular. It was a three-day outdoor music and dance festival with five different stages and performers from all over the world. I hung out with Pam, her husband Peter, and brother Tom. Tom and I had enjoyed a little fling before my road trip but soon realized we were better as friends. We all took in the sights and sounds of the day and into the magic of the night. The warm southern hemisphere air was filled with the sounds of South America and music from the three other continents. One afternoon, I was sitting on the grass listening to a band and right next to me was the actor Guy Pearce wearing a blue singlet and long cotton sarong. He was a world away from Hollywood. I am not a star-struck person by any means, so I just casually said to him, "Hello, I thought your role in *LA Confidential* was superb." He shrugged and thanked me politely but clearly just wanted his privacy and to enjoy the music.

Tom sent me off in style with a lovely dinner and wine on the beach. It was near the pub that a piano scene from the movie *Shine* with Geoffry Rush was filmed. It was based on the life of talented pianist David Helfgott, who suffered a mental breakdown and spent years in institutions. That fact did not interest me. It was the way he played *Flight of the Bumblebee*. Now, that was insane.

I left for Sydney which would be my destination before flying home. Again, I was timely with travelling. It was the infamous Sydney gay pride parade. What a sight to behold! Hundreds of thousands of people lined the streets to see the gay floats, dancers, and flamboyant entertainers strut their stuff shamelessly. I met fun gay guys and hung out at the Judgement Bar before the parade began. Then, I just wandered up and down the streets looking for a good vantage point. At one in the morning, I met a friendly Irish fellow who took a shine to me. I was giddy and could have listened to his lovely rolling accent all night long.

We ended up having sex in the middle of a deserted street on a bench.

For the next few days, I played tourist again by visiting the opera house one last time and having a Shirley Valentine moment on Bondi Beach. I was completely satisfied and at peace with my Australian journey. I have Wanderlust. I am not Paul Coelho, Elizabeth Gilbert, or even Daisy Duck. I am me.

Insomnia

What do you do when you can't sleep?

I returned home to Calgary, Canada in mid-March, back to my condo, cat, and an overwhelming feeling of uncertainty. What does one do after a year of Disney On Ice and travelling the entire continent of Australia? The first thing I did was watch CBC – the Canadian Broadcast Corporation. The next activity I did was cross-country skiing in the Rocky Mountains and Kananaskis Country. The third thing I did was look for a job. My sister Charlotte continued to live with me for a few months as she was struggling with work as well. We were both running out of money.

In the spring, I landed a job as a waitress/server at a high-end restaurant called the River Café on Prince's Island Park. During my orientation, I met Mary from the Maritimes but originally from Calgary. She was yet another fiery redhead with a wicked sense of humour to match. We connected immediately and are still best friends to this day.

Summer was the high season at the River Café, so we worked our butts off, making great cash and partying after work with our fellow servers. I rollerbladed to and from work, down the hills of Bankview, along the bike trails by the Bow River, and then onto the island. It would do the same back at eleven in the evening. I had a lot of energy and was in optimal shape. I also learned all about wine, food, and the nuances of being a high-end salesperson. It wasn't that difficult. You connect with the customer personally, give them what they need, and up-sell with dessert and after-dinner drinks like port, brandy, or dessert wine. A server can increase sales by fifteen percent, which in turn increases your tips.

In the fall, I decided to go back to University and study Kinesiology, Sports Psychology, and Physiology. I was nervous about being an "older student." I found myself being quite annoyed with the younger ones. I did not want to waste my money or time. The studies were challenging, especially statistics and physiology. The former, I couldn't have cared less about. The latter was extremely interesting. I was fascinated by the physiology of the different systems of the body. One professor said, "You could spend a lifetime studying endocrinology and still be baffled by it." Psychology was textbook and clinical. In some ways, I was a square peg trying to fit in a round hole. Or is it a round hole in a square peg?

In October, I felt physically and emotionally

stressed. I had school, mid-terms, skating, waitressing, and family coming for Thanksgiving. To top it off, I went to a chiropractor and found out I was a gimp. We carefully studied my X-rays and discovered that my "straight neck" was causing mega problems in my back. Also, one shoulder was two inches lower than the other and my hips were all out of wack. Dr. Kelly said "trauma" was the cause. Could it be from being dropped on my head in pair skating? How about when I fell a trillion times performing a double axel jump? My muscles and fascia around my spine were screaming at me. Dr. Kelly said it would take a year of treatment. What is a year in a lifetime of stress on my body?

For the first time in my life, I scored fifty-two percent on an exam. I was devastated but I knew exactly what had happened. My heart was pounding and my breathing was shallow right before the exam sheet was placed on my desk. I couldn't read the multiple-choice, convoluted questions properly. My eyesight went blurry. I panicked looking at the clock and started guessing at questions. It had been an hour of pure hell.

In that first year, I had my doubts about university and my future. Did I really want to do my master's degree? Did I really want to be a psychologist? Would I be able to sink my whole heart and soul into it?

I missed the feeling of being committed to something with energy and passion.

In my second year, a devastating event happened in New York. September 11, 2001. I went to school and realized that the news had spread all over the campus on televisions. I was stunned and kind of oblivious, not really believing it was all happening. By November, I began fighting my own internal war. I stopped sleeping properly and had disturbing dreams about being suffocated by dark clouds and the end of the world. I tried phoning my dad in my dream to cry out "help me" but I couldn't get out the words. The sky was falling and was close to my head. In December, I went home for Christmas and remember being incredibly sad. I went back to Calgary flooded with feelings of abandonment and fear.

My sleep patterns got worse. I had trouble concentrating, especially in my horrible statistics class. After three months of not sleeping properly, I had a panic attack at school. My heart was pounding most of the time and I had this perpetual lump in my throat. I didn't know what was happening to me. I made my way home and called my friend Geoff in a panic. He was going through a tough time himself as his father had just suffered a heart attack and he was leaving a dental practice to start his own from scratch. He told me to come over to his place. I somehow made my way there and he gave me a Valium. I slept through the night, for the first time in months, but it was fitful, and I was still in a weird fog-like state. By morning, I called my dad in tears asking him, "Do you remember when I was little, and I slept in between yours and mom's beds? Did you think I was a beautiful skater?" My father was confused and completely thrown off-guard. He didn't know what to say. I took a shower and hoped that the water would wash away the awful feeling that encompassed my body. It did not. Geoff asked, "What are you going to do?" I had no response.

It was clear that I was in a deep dark hole of depression. It was the worst episode I had ever experienced. My sister did not know what to do with me. I went over to her apartment and laid on her bed, wishing that I would die. She suggested medication and I yelled out, "I don't need antidepressants!" The truth was, I did not know anything about them, and they scared the hell out of me. I continued to teach skating part-time and remarkably finished the school year. How I made it through finals, I did not know. I dropped out of statistics one month before it finished. Numbers and graphs baffled me beyond belief. It was devastating.

Finally, I got the help that I needed. My dear cousin Rob had suffered from depression all his life and took me to his doctor. The doctor put me on antidepressants which I called "brain food" and some sleep medication. What a relief it was but it took a few weeks for the medication to work. Even then, it was a painfully slow process. I remember one night I went to a movie with my cousin and in the middle of it had a panic attack. I turned to him and said, "I think I need to go to the hospital." He, my sister, and Paul accompanied me to the hospital and waited for hours. I finally saw a doctor and he said there was nothing wrong with me. I was sent home in the wee hours of the morning. I remember seeing the sunrise and hoping that there would be brighter days ahead.

I was barely functioning. I had no appetite and lost weight. A few times, I stayed in bed, took sleep medication, and call my sister in a panic saying, "Give me a reason to get up." The days seemed long and foreboding. Occasionally, Charlotte and Paul would come over to my place and take me for a walk. When they left, that same feeling of abandonment washed over me.

In the spring, I went to the Calgary Counselling Centre and was set up with my new counsellor who turned out to be my saviour and guardian angel. In our first meeting, I told her what I had been going through and I asked her, "Can you help me?"

"Yes," she replied, "but you will be doing most of the work." Making it to counselling every week for two-hour sessions was a feat unto itself. I have never worked so hard at anything in my life. Gayle and I went to very painful places in my childhood. I cried an ocean of tears. I went back into the dark, hoping and praying that there would be a glimpse of light. I went back to that lonely church basement in Weyburn where I practised piano. I went back to the rides home in the car with my mom and then returning to a lonely home in a place where young girls should not be alone. Every week, I lost a little bit of myself to the darkness. How can one person carry around so much sadness? Why couldn't I just get over it? Gayle used a psychotherapy technique called EMDR (Eye Movement Desensitization and Reprocessing). We would go back to a painful memory, feel, and describe it as she tapped back and forth on my thighs. The idea was to restructure neural pathways in my brain from emotionally traumatic experiences into a more positive state of mind. It was a long, arduous process of recovery.

In the summer, I was working at a diner that a friend owned. I had trouble remembering things, which was challenging for a waitress. One night, I couldn't remember a friend's name. I broke into tears and fled into the bathroom. The manager came in, consoled me, and told me to take all the time I needed. I was frustrated and anxiety-riddled most of the time.

I lived every day in the darkness of my mind. I sucked on ice cubes to relieve the lump in my throat. In the evening after work, I would drive to my swimming hole by the river. I took off my clothes and plunged in to wash the depression off. For a few moments, in the dark of the water and the shadow of the moonlight, I felt nothing. I felt a kindred spirit in the moon. It was watching over me, smiling and encouraging me to go on. One day, I stood out on my balcony and let the rain wash over my body, hoping that it would also wash away the pain and darkness. Again, for a few moments, it worked.

How can I describe the illness of depression? I believe no one can understand it until they go through it. It is like being buried in snow or slow suffocation. You are in a dark forest, running through the rabbit trails, feeling lost with no glimpse of light. It is drowning in stormy seas, yet I chose to grab onto the life raft. When does it all end? Is it true that time heals? Yes, it is with the help of medication, counselling, and self-nurturing. In my experience, it takes about a year.

I learned to soothe myself when I felt the pain of abandonment. I would sob and sob until I could barely breathe and then I would talk myself out of it and repeated the words "You are going to be all right, you are going to be all right." I practiced self-care, which meant everything from good food, supplements, walks, yoga, long baths, sleep, journaling, music, and movies. I asked for help when I needed it. I leaned on family and friends to coach me through the rough patches.

In counselling, we worked on my core beliefs. A bigger core belief could be compared to the palm of your hand and then all these sub core beliefs radiate out through the fingers. A big one was that I was not good enough. All my life, I was judged in a most unforgiving sport. I pushed myself harder all the time and still, I believed that it wasn't good enough. What is enough? I can only guess that many young, high-performance athletes feel the same way. To this day, I am a high achiever but what I do IS enough.

I was an extremely outgoing, vibrant young lady, but during my depression, I was sullen, withdrawn and had panic attacks around people. The mind and body are so intimately connected. One cannot always help but influence the other. I physically felt the disease in my throat, stomach, and heart. The throat signified the challenge of speaking and expressing my truest and innermost feelings; the stomach signified the digestion of the painful times of my life, the lonely times that I could not process as a child; the heart, an organ of love and acceptance. How do you love yourself and have compassion for others when there is a dark cloud over you? I looked my depression straight in the eye and loved it for what it was; I learned to love and accept it for what it was, and then I put it on a shelf for a while. I did the same with fear. It takes a big, open, courageous heart to do this.

Slowly but surely, after a year of treatment, I began to feel more like myself. The clouds lifted, parted, and glimpses of sun entered my life again. In the fall of 2002, I finished my counselling with Gayle. It was time for me to leave the nest. I continued to work at the diner and I gradually got my confidence back. An organic food sales guy named Clay visited the diner regularly and ordered coffee all the time since he was their distributor. I soon realized that it was not the coffee he wanted. It was me he was pursuing. As I healed, my flirtatious side came out again. We started dating and once again, I yielded to falling in love. It was a long and drawn out tumultuous affair. He was right in the middle of a divorce and wasn't ready for a relationship. We broke up and got back together several times. It was one drama after another. I wouldn't give up. My friends all began to lose patience with me and the whole situation.

During the good times, we hung out at my place and I cooked and made us his excellent organic coffee every morning. We laid in bed looking out the window at the bottle pickers going "clickety-clack" up and down the street. We had a "Scrabble bath" together. I put the ironing board across my big tub, and we drank wine while soaking and thinking of clever words. He bought me gifts and called my place the "Lizzada," kind of like the Ramada. How could he give up such an amazing woman? He said, "You are not a girlfriend, you are a wife." Yet, he kept repeating, "I am not ready for a relationship." He wanted the best of both worlds — me and his freedom. What the hell were we doing? I was not listening. I heard what I wanted to hear and saw what I wanted to see.

During my depression and beyond, I found a yoga practice that suited me. It was Ashtanga yoga flow at a pioneering studio in Calgary called Yoga in Motion. I went every day to help me cope with my illness, anxiety, and loneliness. Yoga is awesome for the mind and body, but it is also a sacred place to connect with people of all ages. I volunteered at the studio for a free membership and then landed a part-time job as a receptionist. I did yoga in the park and studio, looked after my flowers, and had picnics at the swimming hole. What a beautiful summer of leisure, play, and recovery. I felt like a child again. Even with my social anxiety, I went to the Calgary International Folk Festival on Prince's Island Park. The air was filled with the smell of curry, burgers, and sugared donuts. I remember the stirring voice of Jane Siberry singing *Calling All Angels*. I looked up at the crescent moon smiling down on me and sighed with relief.

I took Clay to one of my favourite spots called Seebe cliff jumping. It is one hour west of Calgary and a gorgeous rocky view of the icy cold, glacial-washed, blue and green Bow River. We had a picnic and courageously jumped off a five-meter jump. I took a picture of Clay with his arms out like the people that painfully jumped from the towers in New York. His arms hit the water with a smack. Clay took a photo of me leaping off the rock in mid-air. Maybe I was flying or hovering like a hawk in the wind.

In the fall, I volunteered for the Calgary International Film Festival and spent many a day watching films. Clay told me I was living the life of a rockstar. It was a wonderful time of freedom, change, and growth. I wrote Clay a "Dear John" letter and he threw it down without opening it. We continued to have an on-and-off-again relationship. My sister had a few people over for cocktails. Clay and I were on the couch cracking jokes and shamelessly flirting with each other. Charlotte said, "I am going to have to throw water on you two." Our relationship was passionate but the expression "wrong timing" came to mind.

I continued to work at the yoga studio, learning the day-to-day operations of the business. To pay the bills, I landed a job at the Saddledome in the restaurant for the Calgary Flames games. It was good cash but not what I wanted to do for the rest of my life. I had much higher aspirations for my next career. The next chapter would prove to be the most ambitious and productive time of my life.

Create

Don't stay on the surface water for too long.
Plunge in and watch the ripple effect.

My best friend David from Victoria, British Columbia said, "Lizzie, keep your eye on the prize." In the fall of 2003, I looked up at the stars on top of a ten-thousand-foot-high mountain, almost touched them, and realized there was something bigger out there for me. What was it? The half-moon with a cold haze enveloping it cried out, "Passion, passion! You need this in your life, so go out and create it."

On a cool November night, I walked to the Hillhurst arena, which is the coldest rink in Calgary, to watch Clay play hockey. Clay was flattered I was there. What guy wouldn't want a sweet assed girl in the stands watching him skate? After the game, he invited me to the tacky upstairs bar to have a beer with the boys. I felt flattered. What gal wouldn't want a pack of breeder boys surrounding her, looking adorable and cute? Afterwards, we went back to my place and couldn't keep our hands off each other. We had yet another night of lovemaking and "bath talk." I told him about the moon speaking to me and how on one hand I felt like a goddess that was strong, confidant, free, and on the other hand, a vulnerable little girl that just wanted to be loved. He echoed my own words and said, "Lizzie, you need love and passion in your life."

I shared my words of wisdom by responding with, "Clay, you need to stop running and just be. Live for the moment without grief for the past and fears for the future." Perhaps I needed to take my own advice. An entrepreneur was brewing inside of me, just like Clay. By December first, I knew exactly what I needed to do, and it didn't involve a man at all.

The yoga studio I was working for during my period of recovery from depression was failing. The owner was going crazy—literally. He would show up sporadically and lost his train of thought and words during classes. He laid on his back speechless in the reception area of the studio. It was clear to me that he had a mental illness. The once-thriving studio was now losing money fast. I felt compassion for him but what could I do? I had just recovered myself from crippling depression and he had his own battles to face. One of the yoga teachers was waiting in the wings to buy the studio. It had crossed my mind, but I thought, "I could do better, and I have always wanted to start from home plate. I mean, who wouldn't want to hit a home run?"

I bought my condo for a wing and a prayer in 1996 and by 2003, I had a good sum of equity in it. I decided to start the first yoga and pilates studio in downtown Calgary called Core Yoga + Pilates Inc. The first order of business was joining the Alberta Women Entrepreneurs (AWE) and getting my very own business coach. I met her once a week and she taught me everything from creating a business plan to financing and marketing. She was amazing and my learning curve was high. It was fall and my goal was to open in February 2004. I was a business planning machine.

I found space myself in a one-hundred-year-old character building just kiddy corner from the studio that I had worked at. I immediately saw its potential. The next two months were a flurry of activity. I pulled out all the feathers in my cap. A colleague from Disney on Ice was an interior designer and I got him on board. Together, we designed the interior of a 2400 square foot space complete with skylights, hardwood floors, red brick, and high ceilings. It was a gorgeous raw space just waiting for some tender loving care. We designed a reception area with built-in comfy, but contemporary seating, a ten-foot custom made reception desk and avocado green walls that were vibrant yet had a healing appeal. There were two dressing rooms and a massage room with a west-facing window. As it came together, every day was like Christmas. It was the most exciting, creative project I had ever taken on.

For the next three months, I woke up early and wrote my ideas and game plan. There were leases to negotiate and signage to design plus teachers to hire. My good friend Natalie was a graphic artist and did an incredible job of designing my logo. Clay came through for me by informing me that his young assistant James was a self-taught website designer. I was his first client and he completed a spectacular website for under five hundred dollars. When I viewed it for the first time, I cried.

In January, I took possession of the space and my dear brother Mark came from Kelowna to graciously donate his time to build walls. What would I have done without him? I organized a painting party with a group of friends because we had some big walls to paint. The studio was a deep orange and bright yellow. It was energizing and vibrant. My cousin Rob donated office furniture and his partner helped me with the computer programming. In less than two months, it all came together. I did guerrilla marketing and handed out about three hundred business cards with a free class on the back to the businesses in a five-block radius of Core.

I was open for business on February 9, 2004.

It was one of the most exciting days of my life. My enthusiasm combined with the beautiful space made it easy to sell memberships. Remarkably, I had a core group of clients in a noticeably short period. Timing and diligence are important in business—so is a fantastic product. I finished the massage room with a soft wool carpet and a coat or two of an earthy red-brownish paint. I had created a sublease and increased revenue straight away.

A month later, I planned an open-for-business celebration. I hired a percussion band with a group of guys I affectionately called the "Bongo Boyz." They played during yoga class and afterwards for a couple of hours into the evening. I gave out door prizes, catered food, and drinks. It was an exciting day and there was a stupendous turn-out of clients new and old.

I scheduled a weekly print advertising and marketing scheme that worked. I learned how to work with graphic artists for advertising and promotion. I was also a media whore and a shameless self-promoter. In that same month, I had a picture and write up in the Open for Business section of the *Calgary Herald*. Being proud, I sent the article home to the folks.

In the first year, I hosted several parties. In May, I was turning forty. Inspired by the movie *Amadeus*, I hosted a Louis the Fourteenth theme party. I hired a friend who was in the catering business. We planned a five-course dinner with a French theme. I biked down to Theatre Calgary and rented costumes. The servants even wore costumes. There were extravagantly coloured and tailored dresses with plunging necklines and corsets. There were puffy shirts and cossets for the men. I invited ten of my dearest and closest friends.

Core was transformed into a seventeenth-century castle complete with candelabras, flower arrangements with plumes and feathers, and a table setting fit for a king or queen. I wore a red and black gown with a built-in push-up brassiere. I had feathers in my curly locks and bright red lips with dramatic seventeenth-century make-up on my face and eyes. I looked like Marie Antoinette before the peasants cut off her head. My escort Geoff came over and duck taped my breasts up, sporting cleavage. He looked like Louis the Fourteenth.

It was an extravagant evening, to say the least. One of the caterers said, "I wanted to put on a bathing suit and dive right in." Everyone ate and danced the night away. We played musical chairs as I was waltzed around the studio. My feet felt like they were a foot off the floor. Candelabras and wax fell over and glasses were broken. The caterers scolded us, but we just laughed them off.

The losers of the game had to go onto the streets and bring a few commoners to the party. My crazy catering friend Aaron bribed young boys to come up to the third floor in our den of debauchery. They were flabbergasted but managed to fit in as the bartender poured them drinks. The night felt like it would never end. I was a drunken mess. When everyone had left the party, I felt a wave of abandonment fill my gut. I got a ride home with Mary and her husband Steve and crashed on the couch. It was nice to be taken care of. *'I am saved.'*

Party number three took place for the summer solstice. We had a big fusion class with live percussion and dancing afterwards. Again, we served food, wine, and sangria. It was a great kick-off to summer. In August, I took some time off and went to visit my island boys. My good friend and his partner lived in a beautiful house in Victoria and it was my place of refuge. I slept, read, and rested in their garden and occasionally, I heard, "Lizzie, can we bring you a cocktail?" *Saved again.*

The end of summer was a busy time for the business and I prepared for fall with website updates, marketing schemes, and business plans. My main concern was planning Mom and Dad's fiftieth wedding anniversary and family reunion with Charlotte. We hosted it at the studio and the whole clan came. Hearing my mom and dad walk down the hallway to the studio was the most exciting moment of my life. They were astonished as they strolled into the reception area. We greeted them with flowers (red roses for love and yellow for friendship), an elegant white wedding cake decorated with roses, a bar and a studio set up for a lovely dinner. My sister Charlotte and I put together a video of Mom and Dad's life together—the courtship, the babies, the grandchildren, and life in Radville. My dad made a beautiful speech at the dinner and spoke of how Mom had held the family together. My oldest brother made another impromptu speech about growing up in Radville and I had tears in my eyes. By the time we showed the video on the big screen, I was balling. My mom talked about the whole event for months.

By Christmas, I was exhausted. Although, December is my favourite time of year and what would it be without a party? What is it with me and parties? Perhaps I hid my loneliness behind them, surrounding myself with people. Maybe I was Mrs. Dalloway.

The reception area and studio were festively decorated with little white lights and a Christmas tree. I put on my reindeer antlers and ruby red nose and pranced around the studio pulling a wagon full of gifts. We had live percussion and spot dances where the music ended as yoginis froze in anticipation of spontaneous gift-giving. I closed the studio for a few days between Christmas and New Year's and spent the holidays with my Charlotte and Paul. I slept most of the time, getting up only to eat, drink, and bathe.

Looking back on the first year of business, I often thought, *'How can a little gal from Radville, Saskatchewan be so damned lucky? How can I carry such happiness?'* My heart felt like it was going to burst—but it didn't.

Year two of the business flew by with all its challenges and ups and downs. I used the media to my advantage repeatedly with an article in *Fast Forward*, a weekly newspaper, and an appearance on City TV with my Core Kids Yoga program. I and four little cherubs performed some yoga and I answered questions about the program. It was a brilliant concept. The kids do yoga while the parents sip organic herbal tea in the lounge and then they switch while the parents get their class and the kids do crafts and reading in the lounge supervised by the yoga teacher. Everything was taken care of.

Financially, the business was doing well and growing. There were challenging months though where I had to be creative and do some guerrilla marketing. But, if it were easy, wouldn't everyone have their own business? A new landlord took over the building and re-measured my square footage. There was an increase in both the space and my monthly payments. I found out that it was legal and had to deal with it.

My business adviser informed me that I would just need to sell a few more memberships to cover the cost. Eventually, the extra cost was absorbed. The good news was that the landlord got things done. The front entrance and stairwells were all redone. You never get a second chance at a first impression. Potential customers would walk into a clean and professional-looking building.

In year two, I had fewer parties as they require planning, energy, and have extraordinarily little return, except in my own pleasure. I focused on other opportunities in the corporate world. I facilitated health workshops targeting oil companies. They were lunch and learn presentations explaining the importance of yoga in the workplace. It was brilliant and slowly but surely, I built the business outside of its walls. The brochures read "Corporate Yoga." It was a brilliant and unprecedented campaign.

In year three, I once again had many media opportunities. I had a brilliant two-page spread in *Swerve Magazine* with a picture of a coffee cup looking like Starbucks that read "Yoga Lattes." The other page featured me doing an upside-down yoga pose. I also wrote an article for a national woman's business magazine. It was another two-page spread complete with pictures of clients doing yoga at the studio, a backgrounder, and my written words about the health benefits of yoga, Pilates, and "fusion" classes. We had a spot-on City TV again, this time with adults doing yoga. They performed and I was the spokesperson. I seemed to be a natural. I thought about going into television, but the universe had something else in store for me.

I continued to take my yearly trip to Victoria. It was like a cleansing of the body, mind, and spirit. I was surrounded by the ocean, flowers, and green. Of course, my island boys went to great lengths to spoil me. It was like going home. My best friend David and I would take our traditional adventure hikes. We would go to the Sooke Potholes and swim naked in the freshwater falls. We explored ocean beaches and had picnics of homemade wine and scrumptious snacks. We went to a little lake tucked away in the trees with a dock, laid on our air mattress and floated on the still water.

In the evenings, David, Paul, Bruce, and I met in the hot tub surrounded by the magic of their garden. The air was filled with sounds of seagulls and floatplanes. The air smelled delicious. We talked of travel, dreams, and boys. I was lucky to be a girl surrounded by fawning gay boys, once again.

In June, I got out the "party barge," which was a big, square, green raft. Typically, my buddies and I floated down the Elbow River with cocktails and a gorgeous view of the most expensive houses in Calgary. One hot day, my girlfriend and I started at about one in the afternoon. By three o'clock, big black ominous clouds flew in from the west and suddenly we were right in the middle of a hailstorm. We were on the Elbow River, which can be surprisingly fast under the surface. I jumped out of the boat and miraculously pulled us to shore. We perched ourselves under a fence like little birds as two inches of hail fell around us. Finally, it stopped, and we found ourselves soaking wet in the backyard of an expensive property. No one was home so we warmed up in their back porch living room with fuzzy, warm blankets. We emptied the boat of the accumulated ice and off we went down the river.

In year three of the business, I felt like I was on an emotional roller coaster. The honeymoon was over, and I had waves of frustration and loneliness throughout the year. I tried everything from dating services and online dating. It was not a pleasant experience, to say the least. The positive about online dating was the practice of writing, reading, and getting down a paragraph or two about who you are and what you want. It's a good exercise for anyone. The bad news was men, and sometimes women, can lie about age, looks, weight, career, and "I love hiking and walks on the beach." I met a man on Plenty of Fish at a pub who looked shifty from the get-go. He asked, "Would you like a drink?" He went to the bar and I never saw him again.

I had waves of longing for a relationship and a baby. This went on for several years. I was in my early forties and I felt my time was running out. I even considered asking my gay friends to father a baby. My mom asked, "If you had a husband and family, would you have accomplished your goals and lived your dreams?"

In the spring of 2007, I decided to take ten days off and go to Maui. It had been a dream of mine and I made it happen. I stayed at a hostel in Paihia which was nothing fancy but who cares when you are in the middle of paradise? I strolled through the town, ate lovely meals at good restaurants and hung out on the beaches. I met an interesting older fella on a nude beach, and he invited me for an outing with him and his girlfriend. He was fifty-nine and she was thirty. They drove me to a nude beach called "Little Beach." It was a Sunday afternoon and traditionally there was drumming and dancing. I was all too familiar with these activities and the only difference was there were a beautiful beach and naked people. I met a local, originally from South America, who offered to be my tour guide of the island. He seemed safe and kind enough, so I agreed. He was to pick me up at the hostel the next day. I waited but there was no South

American fellow in sight. An older fellow who was staying at the hostel noticed that I was waiting outside with my luggage. I told him about my predicament and my quest to get to the other side of the island. He offered to drive me. I accepted. He was an annoying, chain-smoking, mainland American who seemed to take a liking to me. I was grateful for the ride but was soon irritated by him. We parted ways in Lahaina.

In the historic town of Lahaina, I stayed at a bed and breakfast owned by an artist and his girlfriend. He was a photographer named Pierre and I felt very much at home there. The town was full of art dealers and shops along the waterfront. It was a tourist haven with a hustle and bustle to it. I explored the town, went out for dinners along the ocean and pondered the question, *'Is this weird for a single girl to be in one of the most romantic places in the world?'*

I made the mistake of checking out Pierre's computer and showing him my website. It was a big mess and I couldn't figure out why. I called the studio and my assistants, Sophie and Bob, tried to work the problem without me there. I tried to forget about it since I was on holiday and really couldn't do much about it. My flight home was delayed for a day, so I found myself back at Pierre's, back to the beach, and then the airport. Made it to Los Angeles and then my flight home was delayed for the day. Finally, I made it home to Calgary and went straight to host a health workshop for a company. I was exhausted. I needed a vacation from my vacation.

I found myself back at the studio still burnt out and emotional. The holiday hadn't made my problems go away. I sat at my desk and cried uncontrollably. My friend Sophie consoled me and I decided to make some changes. I took care of my physical body by taking some good vitamins including adrenal support. I asked for more help and decided to take a month off and only go into the studio twice a week. I looked after my flowers and painted the ceiling in my bedroom. It was a huge job because I had to scrape off the stucco and then paint. Thinking about my dad, I thought, *'There is nothing like manual labour to set the soul straight.'*

I went back to my counsellor Gayle and it was like seeing an old friend. We talked for two hours about my recent accomplishments and challenges. I told her about my dream of having a partner and child. With the power of intention, I manifested a man. He was the brother of a client that I had known for a few years. He was married so I did not pay any attention to him. He was going through a divorce and in the market for a girlfriend. He lived in Vancouver but spent some time in Calgary. He invited me to Vancouver at the end of July. I decided to work Vancouver into my Victoria trip.

It was my best friend's big fat gay wedding August long weekend. I was excited and nervous to see my Vancouver man again. I was taking a big chance by going to stay with him after just one dinner and emails. We got along marvellously, strolling around David Suzuki's neighborhood and going out for fancy dinners. He said, "I loved every minute." He put me on a float-plane ride to Victoria. I saw countless islands from the air on the Strait of Juan de Fuca. I felt like Meryl Streep in *Out of Africa*.

The wedding was the most elegant that I have ever had the pleasure of witnessing. They had the ceremony in their garden officiated by David's Aunt Nan who was a chancellor in Calgary. David and Paul were stunningly handsome in black and white as they walked arm and arm to the sweet sounds of Nora Jones. I sat on a deck step and bawled through the whole ceremony.

There were a lovely dinner and dance at the Art Gallery of Victoria. David and Paul's bridesmaids made gracious, humorous speeches and the deliriously happy couple had the first dance. When the whirlwind of activities ended, I visited the boys the day they were leaving for their honeymoon. We said our goodbyes and Bruce and I were left at the house to hang out and visit in the hot tub. I fought off feelings of abandonment and loneliness.

I felt better back in Calgary, plunging into fall business responsibilities. I also flexed my teacher muscle again and taught a couple of yoga classes a week. That was extremely rewarding and different from the day-to-day operations of the business. I poured my heart and soul into my students and the return was ten-fold. I taught teenage girls every Saturday morning. This was a challenge as some girls were totally dialled in and others couldn't be bothered. I rose to the challenge by showing the way.

My Vancouver fellow continued to send me love letter emails and planned a trip to Calgary in the fall. We fell in love but there was something not quite right about our relationship. I had the notion that he didn't want children, and that made me incredibly sad. I was terrified to ask him outright for fear that I would upset the apple cart. He invited me on a trip to Maui and I asked myself, *'How could a girl refuse?'* He came to Calgary for Halloween and then off we flew to Los Angeles and then the island.

It was a good trip except for a night we walked on the beach and I dared to ask him about children. He had no interest in having them whatsoever. I broke down in tears and was terribly upset. We decided to let the conversation drop and enjoy the rest of the trip. I knew deep down that I was not being true to myself. I was not in love with him. I could also feel the signs of depression coming on. We flew back to Vancouver. I had planned to stay for a couple of weeks. He went back to work, and I wandered around the city feeling lonely, lost, and abandoned. Each day, I could feel the darkness creep into my body and mind. I felt periods of anxiety and dread. My mood was as dark as the Vancouver clouds hovering over the coastline.

Winter

Pain now is part of the joy then.
Joy now is the pain now and then.

I am in the emergency waiting room at the hospital. It has been six hours. My whole body is shaking from the inside out. Gayle, my old counsellor, has come out to apologize for the wait. She is an emergency psychiatric nurse. I am terrified. My sister fetches me a sandwich. I am sitting in a chair with my knees to my chest rocking and shaking. Eight hours later, they call my name. I am put in a stark room with padded walls and a bed with nothing on it. I wait for another hour. Someone comes in to check my vitals. My sister comes in with me to wait for another hour. I am guessing it is about eleven o'clock at night. She tries to comfort me but to no avail.

Finally, a doctor comes in and asks me all kinds of questions. The big one is, "Are you suicidal?"

I replied in a cracked voice, "I have had thoughts of suicide. I need to sleep and I need something to stop me from shaking." He leaves and assures me that I will sleep tonight and that they will check to see if there is a bed available. A nurse comes in and gives me an Ativan, which is a low-dose sedative. I immediately start to feel better. My sister and I hear screaming and pounding in the next room. Someone brings in a wheelchair and I am wheeled down the hall. I am slurring my words as my forlorn sister says goodbye to me.

It is about midnight and a nurse empties my purse and takes stuff out that I cannot keep. They do more vital tests and take blood this time. I am given some Seroquel, another kind of sedative, and I sleep. I had no idea that it was an anti-psychotic drug. I awaken in a room with another bed beside me, a curtain, and a washroom. The washroom with a shower smells like rank water and cleaning solution. I feel remarkably better after sleeping. I venture out into a big room with a nurses station at one end and a lunchroom at the other. In the middle, there are tables and a couch with a television. It's not bad, as far as I can tell. I venture to the lunchroom and look for a breakfast tray. I have no idea what the procedure is. Eventually, I figure out that everyone has papers with their names and what they had ordered on their tray. I think they ordered one for me.

I was in a three day "short-term" stay psychiatric facility. I saw a psychiatrist once a day for ten minutes. There were psychiatric nurses there to give out the pills and babysit the really messed up people. My sister showed up in the early afternoon with clothes, a yoga mat, and some other personal items. Day one wasn't too bad. I could sign out whenever I wanted to go for walks around the hospital or outside. I was terrified of getting lost in the halls of the hospital so I stuck to a main route to the outside. It was the end of December and the days were cold and short. I was in north-east Calgary, which is like a barren, wasteland of busy car-ridden streets, malls, and dodgy looking people.

I dreaded the impending darkness of the day. It was about four in the afternoon. Dinner was at five. I kept pretty much to myself and wondered how I was going to make it through the evening. I asked the nurse for some paper. She gave me a leftover Christmas stocking with little gifts in it. There was a small journal for me to write in. I could barely write but I managed to scribble a few sentences of how I was feeling. "What is going to happen to me? I am full of anxiety all of the time." At night, I was given a Seroquel that made me kind of dopey. An hour later, I was given a blue sleeping pill that had a bitter, metallic taste to it. With all the money spent on pharmaceuticals, why the hell hasn't someone coated the damned pills with anything else? I laid on my little pillow with a skanky plastic cover and listened to the whirring of a fan. There was no way of opening a window. My roommate was a young girl in her early twenties who laid on her bed and said nothing. I thought she had attempted suicide. The thought had crossed my mind, too.

The next day it was New Year's Eve. The doctor

decided to give me a night's leave as a test drive to see if I could function. I packed up my belongings and waited for my cousin Rob to pick me up in the evening. The nursing desk was very quiet. They gave me my nightly drugs and sent me on my way. I was terrified to go home. That was where the darkness began. I couldn't even listen to my voice messages so Rob played them for me. He left to go to a party and I laid on the couch and watched television. I tried to watch *When Harry Met Sally*. Meg Ryan and Billy Crystal could not get me through that one. I took my drugs and had a fitful sleep. In the morning, I knew I was not able to function alone at home. I could barely get myself dressed.

We had a family meeting at the hospital and my cousin came to pick me up. My best friend Mary met us at the hospital and we sat in on a meeting with my arrogant, egotistical psychiatrist. I sat there shaking and annoyed at his pretentious words. None of what he said made any sense to me or anyone else there. Mary did not take any bullshit and questioned him. I sat in a little ball sobbing, distraught and unable to express myself in words. The psychiatrist suddenly got up, decided to dismiss me from the short-term stay at the hospital, and left the room abruptly. My sister, cousin, and Mary decided that long-term stay was the only option. What could I do? I was very upset but I managed to succumb and I sobbed to Mary, "Someday, I will write about this."

I was transferred to the third floor. I was hopeful that it would be all right. I was roomed with a craggy old lady who just laid in bed all day long with tubes attached to machines to help her breathe. She looked near death. I was surrounded by schizophrenics, bipolar, and depressed people. The first night there, a really messed up young guy bounced his head off the floor and reception desk. It looked like he had done it on purpose. I was terrified. I called my sister and described the scene. I told her there was a piano in the lounge. She imagined me playing it. I went over to it and I couldn't even imagine beginning to play it. There was a man who mumbled to himself and urinated in the lunchroom. *'I can't stay here, I can't stay here.'* My sister was very upset and called Mary for consoling. I was under a voluntary stay. I imagined myself running away and hitchhiking to Saskatchewan. I imagined myself taking a taxi and jumping out the door into traffic. I was living a nightmare with no end in sight.

The only people who came to visit me were Mary, Charlotte, Rob, and a friend named Rose. She offered to help and be a caregiver. I did not want anyone else. There were two phones that forty people used. I imagined that they were covered in germs. The nurses wore rubber gloves. The urination guy wandered around half-naked and talked on the phone like he was a salesman. Maybe he had been one in the past. Some people were there for many months. I sort of befriended an English girl who appeared to be the only "sane" person there. She was almost ready to go home. She offered to make me tea. She knitted to relax. I could not relax. I did not know it at the time, but I was given low dosages of Seroquel, an anti-psychotic, that made me shake all day long. One nurse kept popping them into my mouth, thinking it would help my shaking. It only made me worse. Another nurse from hell commented on my vitamin pills by saying, "Why do you need those, the food is really good here."

'Are you kidding me?' I wanted to tell her what a bitch she was, but I was too out of it to get the words out.

I lost a lot of weight. I tried to do yoga in an office room. That lasted about five minutes. I couldn't concentrate. I tried taking a shower and the water was lukewarm. I called Mary and got her answering machine. I fanatically blurted out, " I cannot stay here, I cannot stay here!" But, where would I go?

Mary had a newborn baby and still managed to drive through horrendous traffic on Deerfoot Trail for an hour north to the hospital. She even offered to take me to the Zoo Lights display with her husband Steve and baby Graham. I was strung out on Seroquel but went anyways. I walked around with them in a daze and went through a maze of flashing lights. I felt dizzy and nearly fainted. They took me back to the hospital.

It was the second week of January. My sister informed me that Mom and Dad were coming. I was in a panic. I want didn't want them to see me that way. My sister and her partner went back to my place to get it ready for my parents. In the hospital, I was allowed outings so I went over to Charlotte's place. I remember taking a hot shower and my head and neck felt so heavy. I could barely wash my hair. When I got out of the bathroom, I was frustrated and blurted out, "I am not going home anytime soon, am I?

Mom and Dad arrived and I felt distraught on the couch. My dad held me for a very long time. I was full of anxiety and shaking all of the time. My mom gave me one of her anti-anxiety pills. They seemed to work. We decided that I should dismiss myself from the hospital and stay with Charlotte. I had an appointment with a new doctor and my parents stayed until that day. I was off the old antidepressants that over stimulated me but I was still on Seroquel and sleep medication.

The days were long and all I wanted to do was stay in bed. I managed to get outside for walks with my dad. Sometimes, we would have dinner at Charlotte's and other times, Mom would make dinner at my place.

It was weird being at home but in a way comforting to know that my folks were there.

How did all of this happen? Is depression inherited? Is it developmental? Is it cyclical? There are many theories. My mom is bipolar and coincidentally suffered an episode at the same time as mine. She managed to hide it very well throughout her life. There were times during the day when she would lay down and rest. We thought it was migraine headaches. Perhaps it was something else. How did she manage to raise seven children in small-town Saskatchewan with a mental illness? How did she cope with the isolation that housewives can feel living on the prairies? My mother bravely endured it.

After a disastrous trip to Maui with the wrong boyfriend, I wandered the streets of Vancouver in November 2007. I could feel myself descending into a tailspin. After two weeks, I returned to Calgary. I knew that I was very sick but had no family doctor and no medication. I was desperate for sleep and I managed to convince my cousin to give me some of his medication. It was a "benzo" and very addictive. I found a new young doctor who was a major piece of work. There are good and bad doctors in this world. She was a family doctor who knew nothing about mental illness. She spent an hour conversing with the pharmacist about medication and then blamed me for taking up too much of her time. She stood over me in the clinic room yelling at me with some kind of eastern European accent. I thought to myself, *'She is a nazi doctor.'* She kicked me when I was down. She kept hiking up an antidepressant called Effexor which consequently made me physically overstimulated all day long. It was a horrible feeling and the only thing that made it go away was sleeping pills. I was up and down like a roller coaster. I had panic attacks at the studio.

Christmas was approaching and every day I had trouble functioning. I spent the holidays with my sister but I did not sleepover at their house. I had trouble remembering one moment to the next. On December twenty-eighth, Mary came over and we went out for Vietnamese food. I was slurring my words. We went back to my place to watch a movie and I was burning up on the couch. I took some medication and Mary slept on the couch. During the night, I got up and took a bunch of Gravol. In the morning, I stumbled down the stairs and said to Mary, "I don't think I am going to make it through the weekend." Mary knew that I was in big trouble. She called my sister and cousin and my old counsellor Gail. I managed to make it to a counselling appointment with Charlotte and Mary. I confessed that I had been contemplating suicide. We did not know what to do. Gail suggested that I go to emergency at the hospital she worked at. We gathered some clothes together and off we went. We did not have much choice at that point.

My parents spent two weeks in Calgary at the beginning of 2008. My mom spent most of her time laying on the couch at my condo struggling with her own depression. Dad spent a whole day with me at my sister's home. We went to my condo and Mom said, "How could you leave me here alone all day?" I was horrified, wracked with guilt yet unable to help her at all.

I saw a new psychiatrist who prescribed a different antidepressant for me that he described as "a cleaner drug" called Cipralex. Medication can only do so much and the rest is counselling and of course, there is the adage "time heals." Time has no meaning for depression. It is like a black hole. It is like being out in a field in the middle of a winter storm surrounded by grey with no light in sight.

The worst of it lasted for several months. I stayed at my sister's for two months and realized that I had to go home eventually. Another friend told me, "Get your power back." I was terrified. Home was where the nightmare had begun. It was where I spent most of my journey in a lonely, hard, seemingly endless turmoil. It was no longer a safe place for me. I decided to take baby steps.

I went home for a few hours at a time to clean, have a cup of tea, and visit my cat. My neighbour and good friend Sophie and her daughter Stella had looked after him. They came into my condo to feed him. He suffered from loneliness and neglect. Before the illness, I loved my cat. During the illness, I couldn't have cared less about him. I couldn't take care of myself, let alone a pet. I continued to see my counsellor Gayle once a week.

Remarkably, the business kept going but it was waning. My friend and yoga teacher Sophie took over while I was away. She did an amazing job. But, the captain of the ship was absent and the ship sailed off course. Sales started to slip and my regular clients began to lose faith in a space that had lost its spark and energy. I went there periodically, did a little administrative work, joined in on a class sporadically, and then went home.

My lease was up at the end of the year and Calgary was at the end of an economic boom. The landlord decided to hike my rent up to more than twice the original amount. With that and my illness, it was clear that I would have to sell the business or just close it. With the help of my business adviser, we tried to sell it. There were no takers because of the increased rent and why would one want to move Core out of the core of downtown? Plus rent was high everywhere.

Giving up my creation was one of the hardest things I have ever done in my life. It was like a death. My heart and soul ached. I began to take more and more sleeping pills to numb the pain. I wouldn't show up to the studio and at times during the day, I was strung out and numb from drugs. The situation only became worse.

In the fall, I liquidated all the assets of the studio. It was like selling off one piece of my soul at a time. It took about a month to finish. My friends came to the studio and took stuff that I could not sell. I sent off one last email to my clients explaining the situation. Somehow, that act of truth lifted a weight off my shoulders. I locked the door, said goodbye to a space that had given me such joy for four years, and that was that.

I had lost the business, my identity, my baby, and my heart. I sunk into oblivion. I took more and more drugs. I went to all kinds of doctors and walk-in clinics to get more when I ran out. I used my acting skills, lying about leaving my medications in Saskatchewan and being very distraught about having no medications and being sleep deprived.

By December 2008, I felt like I had three choices: suicide, hospital, or go home to my parents in Radville, Saskatchewan. I chose the latter. I flew home to stay for an indefinite amount of time. It was a bittersweet time. It would likely be the last time that I would spend a few months with my parents. Perhaps I was making up for lost time. They took good care of me. It was a bitterly cold winter. I spent my time reading, walking, and occasionally cross-country skiing. There were hundreds of deer in the fields and I felt like I connected to them. They buried themselves into little snow nests to stay warm. I felt like joining them. When they ran out of food in the fields, they made their way into my mom and dad's garden. I learned a lot about deer that winter.

I paid attention to wildlife. One day, I was driving home from my cousin's farm and a buck and deer were running alongside me in the field. Another time, my folks and I were driving home from Regina and we spotted a wolf walking straight down the middle of the highway. I told myself that those were good signs.

Christmas came and went. I spent it quietly with my folks. Mom made a huge turkey dinner and I helped. It was minus thirty degrees for several weeks in a row so the best thing to do was hunker down and eat comforting winter food. On New Year's Eve, I went outside to say hello to the moon and stars. It was as crisp, clear, and cold as could be. Even though I was lost, it was a significant way to welcome the New Year.

I saw Mom and Dad's doctor in Radville. She

was very good and I was comforted by the fact that my mom was well taken care of. I took drugs off and on. One night, my mom asked why I needed more sleeping pills.

"Because I am hooked on them." I sobbed in her arms. She just held me and patted my back. She suggested that I have a bath to feel better. She had her own demons and troubles to deal with. She did the best she could. I guessed that taking care of me gave her a purpose. We played Scrabble almost every day and watched a movie every night. It was a special time for us. We needed each other and became good friends.

I went skating with my dad one morning at the old rink. I felt like a foreign body attached to my legs. Afterwards, I felt nauseous. We went home, I took a pill and went back to bed. It was not a good exercising experience. Two months passed and I knew that the longer I stayed, the harder it would be to go. One morning, my mom and I had a blowout. For a few years before my illness, my mom had been losing her hearing. She wore a hearing aid. In the mornings, she did not wear it. I took pills behind her back. That morning, she knew I was up to something and chased after me. I locked the bedroom door and she banged on it, demanding that I open it. That was our one and only fight. It was time for me to go. My dad drove me back to Calgary. I was scared to be left alone. My dad stayed for a week and did some chores around the condo. One morning, he got up early, kissed me on the cheek while he thought I was sleeping, and then he was gone. I felt abandonment anxiety coming on and took more pills. That continued for the next several months.

I had to find a job. I did not have a clue where to begin. I targeted coffee shops. I lasted a week at one and three days at Starbucks. I was full of performance anxiety and had trouble remembering things. It was a horrible experience. It was spring and I felt like I had nothing to look forward to. I had no job and no purpose. I had lost my confidence and self-worth.

I attended addictions counselling to address my problem with prescription drugs. It did not seem to help. In August, my doctor-hopping and abuse of prescription drugs finally caught up to me. My doctor cut me off from the sleeping pills. I went cold turkey and then I went through withdrawal. I spent the day shaking in bed and phoned 911. An ambulance came and took me to hospital number two. I waited for hours again in a little enclosed room. I laid on the bed with my hospital gown on and shook. I asked a nurse for an anti-anxiety pill. It helped me stop shaking for a while. Eventually, I got my clothes and purse and just walked out of the hospital without seeing a doctor.

It was a blessing to be drug-free except for the anti-anxiety pills.

By mid-September, I had found a job at a wine boutique. It was not far from my home and I worked three days a week. Slowly by surely, my confidence returned. It was hard work and I ran the store by myself for the most part. My boss treated me well and I was good with the customers.

For Halloween, I ventured out with my friends to a party and dance. I met a fellow there and gave him my phone number. He was a friend of my friends so I felt safe. I needed to test the waters again. We went out a few times but we did not really connect. I danced around the apartment singing Anne Murray and Nelly Furtado's "Cheer up, sleepy Jean, oh what can it mean to a daydream believer and a homecoming queen." He looked at me like I was on another planet.

In December, I had my first Christmas party in two years. I hosted a tacky Christmas gift party. It was a big hit. Most of my good friends made it even though it was about minus twenty-five degrees out. I cooked, made a fire, and enjoyed the company of my guests. When everyone left, I felt the pangs of abandonment anxiety and had a big cry. I had started seeing a new male counsellor in November and we addressed that issue and several skeletons in my closet. He was an amazing therapist and we made some progress. One day, he asked me, "Are you addicted to suffering?" That pissed me off. He had hit a nerve and it was time for a change.

Christmas came and I was off to Vancouver Island to visit my sister Charlotte and my island "boyz." Charlotte had moved there a year earlier, and I missed her terribly. I packed up my gifts and tested my confidence in travelling by plane. David, Paul, and Bruce lived on a beautiful acreage complete with a forest, orchard, and an English garden. The house was gorgeous, warm, and welcoming. We drank wine in the backyard around a fire. We decorated a tree and shared lovely meals. It was all very festive yet quiet and relaxing. My friends and sister loved their gifts. I was always better at giving than receiving. A week went by quickly and back home I went. A good friend picked me up at the airport and dropped me off at home. I was prepared this time for those pangs of abandonment anxiety and actually felt pretty good.

In January, I took a nosedive. I was unsatisfied with my job and started calling in sick quite often. I took sleeping pills and stayed in bed for half of the day. I ran out of pills and took twenty-five ibuprofen in a span of a few hours. It wasn't the pills that hurt me, it was the self beating up the self. In the afternoon, I was desperate and called 911. I mentioned the words pills and suicide and an ambulance was at my doorstep in ten minutes. I told them that I was going to be all right and that I did not need to go to the hospital. I had no choice but to go with them. They said, "You can either come quietly with us or we take you by force." A female cop escorted me to my bedroom so I could change. I was calm and submissive by that point.

They took me to hospital number three and it was the best thing that ever happened to me. They let me keep my street clothes on and put me in a comfortable room with a couch. They offered me food. Within two hours, a doctor saw me. After that, a psychiatric nurse spent an hour with me. I couldn't believe it. It was a much different hospital experience. The nurse even followed up by referring an outreach worker to call me in the morning. I was flabbergasted. The universe was smiling down on me and saying, "This is your chance, this is your chance."

I was released from the hospital and my neighbour friend picked me up. I was quiet and calm. The next day, I cried an ocean of tears. I went for a walk and desperately said to myself over and over, "You are going to be all right." My best friend Mary called me and asked, "What happened?"

"I took a bunch of Advil," I replied.

"How many exactly?" Her voice was wavering.

"Twenty or thirty."

She was furious. I could not blame her. Being honest with Mary about my pill-popping nearly killed me. From that moment on, I made a promise to myself. I was not going to dump my crap on friends and family anymore. Enough was enough.

The outreach nurse called me and I felt like she was a special angel sent just for me. She came to my home the next day with kindness and compassion. I called my counsellor and made an appointment right away. I also called my employer and faced the music. He had nothing but good things to say but thought it best that I focus on getting well. I was set free. I called my dad and told him the truth. I had hit rock bottom and I had only two choices: drown or swim. I chose the latter. I grabbed the life raft and held on. From that day forward, nothing would ever be the same again.

ACT II

Savannah

Home sweet home.
But, I will always have Georgia on my mind.

My body wants to make out with young Richard from Texas. His hands are all over me as I straddle him on the bench in front of the Forsythe Park fountain. It is after midnight and I am intoxicated by the warm Savannah air, gobs of dripping Spanish moss hanging off oaks and a *lingering scent of Azalea and Jasmine. We are a wee bit tipsy from the gin and tonics consumed at the Spanish dance club an hour before. He kisses my neck as I brush my lips over his face and press my perky breasts into his chest. His hands are all over my ass and he pleads with me saying, "I want you so bad." I look at him straight in the eye and say in a Scarlet O'Hara voice, "Alas, I want to, but I left my heart in Atlanta." I jump off him and skip around the fountain like a precocious child who has just gotten her way. Dearest Richard hangs his head as he politely walks me back to the pension a few blocks away. I announce, "It is way past my bedtime. Do you know your way back to the hotel?" He assures me that he will be all right as we say our goodbyes. I pause at the door, look back at him as he walks away and think, 'Half the fun of having sex is not having sex.' I am a wickedly, consummate seductress.*

What brought me to Savannah? Well, several reasons but first and foremost — I love the film *Midnight in the Garden of Good and Evil*, directed by Clint Eastwood, starring Kevin Spacey and John Cusack. I was intrigued by the statue of the girl in Bonaventure cemetery balancing a plate in each hand. The 1994 non-fiction book by John Berendt, along with the movie, put Savannah on the world map and skyrocketed his true crime book on the *New York Time's* bestseller list for over four years. Berendt fell in love with Savannah and I was beguiled by it. It was an intoxicating city with countless squares, fountains, statues, graveyards, Baroque fantasy 1890s mansions, and quirky, eccentric people. Berendt said, "Eccentrics are artists who are masterpieces of their own life. They love to gossip — especially about strange people." Here is another fun fact: The Savannah cobblestones are Spanish stones and Spanish moss is not Spanish or even moss at all. It is from the pineapple family. It is native to Mexico, Central and South America, the Caribbean, and the southern United States. Native Americans called it Itla-okla, which means "tree hair." The native women used it for dresses.

I left Atlanta from a hole in the wall bus station. I waited outside and realized that there were quirky, shady characters hanging around who could have been drug addicts or dealers. Not to worry, I was safe on the bus behind a funny black bus driver who played his rooster "cock-a-doodle-do" cell phone ring right by his microphone. He told jokes and a few silly stories with a southern drawl. Three and a half hours of gazing out the window, snacking, napping, and dreaming flew by in a flash. As we pulled into the Savannah bus station, I was so excited, I could have peed my panties.

I left the dubious, no-cabs-in-sight bus station (it is not even on the tourist map) with my pull cart luggage and backpack. I walked in the direction that I thought might have been the city centre. Guessing that

I was going in the direction of the pension, I soon got lost. You see, I was bewitched with every block and in a dreamy, trance-like state. A kind young fellow pointed me to "Hull" street rather than my "Hall" street destination. I didn't give a rat's ass because, everywhere I turned was bloody gorgeous. Finally, after dragging my luggage up and down the streets of Savannah, it was tourists who pointed me in the right direction.

I saw the Savannah International Pension. It is a modest two-storey white house with pastel trim on the corner with the front steps. In the true Savannahian way, there was a note on the door that said, "Back in twenty minutes." I sat on the steps sweating but happy to be home, so to speak. I met the very friendly owner named Brian and his chatty daughter Isabelle. We took care of business and I was shown to my room. It was huge with a fireplace, a large window, an old-style air conditioner, a modest bunk bed, and a closet with a few hangers for my sundresses. There was a comfortable common room along with a small kitchen. I set some Kicking Horse Coffee out for the other guests, thinking they may enjoy some coffee from Canada. *'This is perfect.'*

After a shower in a clawfoot bathtub, I dressed up in my long green sundress, heeled sandals, and green sparkly little handbag and off I went a'walking.

I strolled west towards the late afternoon sun and saw Forsythe Park. There was a fountain there that looked like it was straight from Versailles. The sun sparkled off the water in streaks of light through a canopy of green. I lingered for a while, then I turned north on Bull Street and walked into not just one square, but five—Monterey, Madison, Chippewa, Wright, and Johnson—all utterly beautiful.

Savannah was America's first planned city. General James Oglethorpe, laid the city out in a series of grids that had wide-open streets, squares, and parks intended for town meetings and business. The magnificent fountains and eerie yet welcoming cemeteries came later. No wonder all I wanted to do was walk. City planners of North America—take heed.

I saw City Hall on the right (another landmark) and then... wait for it... the Savannah River waterfront. River Street was known as the warehouse row and supported the cotton industry. It had been abandoned for decades after three yellow-fever epidemics in the nineteenth century and a hurricane. It was rediscovered and put back to use in the 1970s.

I spotted a swanky place called the Bohemian Hotel, liked the name, and ended up on Rocks on the Roof with a spectacular few of the bridge, river, and the changing colours of the sinking sun. Cocktails and small plates on a roof—what could be better? I was in heaven. There was Savannah, in all its charm during the day. Then, there were the nuances of gaslights shimmering off foliage and flowers at night. The air was warm, with a light humidity that awakened the sultry smells of food, earth, spring magnolias, and azaleas. I was drunk with pleasure as I leisurely walked back to the pension. As I took the same route back, I thought to myself, *'It will look entirely different at night.'*

The next two days were filled with more discoveries like the Old Savannah Trolley Tour. There were twenty-two squares and fifteen hop-on and hop-off stops. It was the best bang for my buck. The bizarre trolley drivers told tales of the different landmarks in their southern Savannahian drawl. The stories always included not only history but a little gossip of people dead or alive. I was completely entertained and transfixed by every scene and structure that went by.

I saw the Mercer-Williams house, once home to lyricist Johnny Mercer (*Moon River*) but also Jim Williams. Williams is known as the only individual in the state to be tried four times for the same crime for a grisly murder within the house. On a lighter note, I saw the Juliett Gordon Low birthplace. She founded the American Girl Scouts in 1912. I was awestruck by the Cathedral of St. John the Baptist with its towering, light blue spires and stained-glass windows built in 1876. It was destroyed by fire in 1898 and rebuilt within two years. I saw The Waving Girl statue on East River Street. Her name was Florence Martus and she unofficially greeted ships entering and leaving Savannah port by waving a cloth from 1887 to 1931. From her rustic cottage on Elba Island, Martus would wave a handkerchief by day and a lantern by night. Rumour had it, not a ship of sailors was missed in her forty-four years on watch.

I spoke to Savannahians as I went along, asking questions of the locals and enjoyed the southern politeness of "Yes, Ma'am." I joked with a couple of gay men, spoke with a few nutty tour guides and generally tried to stay out of trouble. However, after an hour or two of exploring the exquisitely beautiful Mercer-Williams house with its 1700s furnishings, I decided to have dinner at The Olde Pink House. It was one of the more than fifty houses Williams restored from 1955 to 1985. I dressed up in a cocktail dress, shawl, and heals, then made my way to Abercorn Street. The restaurant was indeed pink and very closed as a private function was going on. I chatted up the doorman, pretended to be on the guest list and, in true Savannahian style, crashed the party. It was a hob-nob kind of crowd which was not really my scene. However, I stayed long enough for bubbly and canapes.

The next day, I discovered a lovely park and open stage five minutes from my digs. I packed a picnic lunch and laid on the grass in the sun and people-watched. Young artists were drawing and I discovered that they were students of the Savannah College of Art and Design. Sweet. If I studied art and design, Savannah and perhaps Paris would be my choice cities.

The catalyst for my adventure to Georgia was an opportunity that had knocked on my door. A friend and former lover from Atlanta had invited me to meet him for a weekend in Tampa, Florida. I thought, *'Why just Tampa when I could fly back to Atlanta and skip on over to Savannah?'* My adventurous travelling theme apparently must end in "ah."

I had dated Lee back in Calgary in January 1994. He was a blossoming architect preparing to leave for Lillehammer, Norway for the winter Olympics. I was hanging out at the Auburn Saloon, a trendy martini bar in downtown Calgary, with my gay friends who I affectionately labelled the "gay parade." I grew tired of their company so wandered over to a table of men and stated, "I am sick of my gay friends. I hope you are not gay, although all men are until they prove otherwise." The men at the table laughed and I took a liking to one with long wavy hockey hair and mischievous blue eyes. We ended up sharing a cab back to my place. We frolicked in the backseat in a semi-drunken state and I had, shall I say, a sleepover.

I was in awe of the man. He had a studio that he proudly showed off in the old Uptown building on Ninth Avenue in Calgary. He had an oldish house in Inglewood that he and a colleague were restoring. And, the clincher: he was going to the Olympics to build a pin trading center for Coca Cola. Oh yes, he was not bad in the sack as well.

We dated for three months, he slept over at my condo several times, and we crashed a few parties. My dear gay cousin Rob hosted an Academy Awards party every year and rented a large party room at the Westin Hotel. We all dressed up to the nines, drank bubbly, and made caddy, candid remarks about the stars and what they were wearing. That scenario hasn't changed in twenty-five years.

Lee and I also made appearances at my best gay friend's shwanky condo situated beautifully on the eighth floor facing west towards the mountains. Geoff was known as "the dancing dentist" and the "godfather." He was a retired, talented figure skater originally from Craven, Saskatchewan who had partnered young dancing skaters, as a volunteer, in Springbank, Alberta, twenty kilometres west of Calgary. That was where we had met as I was a professional figure skating coach there for three years. Male dancing partners were scarce in Calgary. He was one of the best. Geoff was also and, still is, a successful dentist with his own practice in Calgary. He is a well-to-do, proud, gay man with charm, attitude, and wit. He has a propensity for pleasure and is incredibly generous, too. Some of his friends revered him. I, however, amused him with"Lizzieizms" such as calling him a "silly git" or "twat." Geoff affectionately called me "Apizaleth" (Elizabeth) or "little troll girl."

For my thirtieth birthday, he put beautiful porcelain veneers on my teeth, hiding the gaps between my front teeth and incisors. I'd had three years of braces as a teenager and for some odd reason, my orthodontist removed eight teeth, including my incisors. Apparently, I had a small jaw and my teeth grew into ten-year gaps that made me look like a chipmunk. I remember the pain and pressure on my jaw when the orthodontist had regularly tightened them. Sometimes, when I am stressed, I still have horrible dreams of my teeth falling out. Geoff and his assistant Debbie transformed my teeth on his day off and they were both hungover and reeked of alcohol. I laid back in the dentist's chair and said humbly, "I hope you do your best work like this." He did because when it was all said and done, I could not stop smiling with my pearly whites.

Geoffrey hosted a multitude of fancy dinner parties with plenty of wine and martinis consumed by all. One night, we "fag hags" ended up taking off our blouses and flouncing around in a drunken mess on the floor. Lee thought he had died and gone to heaven. He suggested a threesome with my well-endowed friend Debbie but I refused, stating firmly, "I want you all to myself." He had more than a handful with me and my insatiable sexual, thirty-something appetite.

When the Olympics were over, Lee returned to Calgary and said, "I have some good news and bad news. I have been offered a job with Coca-Cola and I am moving to the States in a month." My heart was broken. I remember driving him to the airport in the rain. I kid you not. It was raining hard like a scene from *The Bridges of Madison County*. We said our goodbyes and I bawled my eyes out on the way home. To cope with my pain, I started running and working out. I entered a Theater Calgary charity ten-kilometre race and won. I still had my running legs under me after all.

Long story short, Lee married, had four kids, divorced, and we hooked up on LinkedIn fifteen years later. We had a telephone, slightly sexual, long-distance relationship for several months. He was living in Buffalo, New York and his ex-wife and children were in Atlanta, Georgia. We reunited in Toronto, Ontario for a three-day sex fest and eating frenzy. It was the dead of winter but who cared? We stayed at his gay brother's lovely downtown condo. His brother was very generous and must have known that Lee had not been laid for a very long time. I bought Ted a lovely bouquet as a thank-you from a market in Cabbagetown. I also accidentally left him a pair of black lace panties somewhere in his condo. I was horrified and he was amused by it. I think he said to Lee, "This is very cliché."

Lee was a recovered alcoholic and I admired him for that. The recovery rate is low and relapse is high. Addiction is a tricky business for anyone at any time. Frankly, I think people can be addicted to anything including drugs, alcohol, nicotine, sex, food, exercise, the internet, cellphones, social media, misery, and so on. Have we not all been guilty of numbing out at one time or another?

I drank wine and he drank sparkling water or sweet tea. We took the subway and streetcar to the Harbourfront Centre by Lake Ontario. We saw a live dance performance at the Arts Center and held hands. I was in seventh heaven. We wined, dined, drank lattes, and had hot sex. Perhaps, someday, I will write a short story called, *Three Days*. But, I digress.

I flew back to Calgary in a kind of la-la-land state of mind. I continued to work at my little garage converted yoga studio in Inglewood and managed events with Candy Consulting Event Management and Promotion. Lee and I continued to have long phone conversations about the National Hockey League playoffs, work, play, and sex. Men are so predictable and confusing all at once. Perhaps they feel the same way about us. However, women talk about their feelings and men bury them. The exception is, of course, most gay men.

Lee had stress about work, money, guilt about alcoholism, his divorce, and separation from his children. Most of the time, I could not figure it out. Sometimes, he spoke in riddles. It was apparent that he was not ready for someone like me, but he still wanted to see me. I was certain he enjoyed the attention and the sex.

In the spring of that same year, three months after our rendezvous in Toronto, we discussed a meeting in Dallas and then planned one in Tampa. Lee was working there for three days and then we would fly to Atlanta because I had every intention of going to Savannah. My good friend Lynn generously donated a shwack of Airmiles for my, "Trying To Establish a Relationship For Lizzie Fund." We spent a couple of hours over wine and a computer planning the trip. Ten days before the get-a-way, Lee pulled the rug out from under me. He emailed me from Buffalo saying things like perhaps meeting me was not a good idea and that Toronto was just a "casual encounter." I was shocked, hurt, and angry. I immediately called my longtime friend Bonita and we tried to make some sense of it all.

Deep down, I knew that Lee was and never would be in love with me. In between the bouts of crying and anger, I realized that I didn't need him at all. I was still me with an abundance of love to give and all the possibilities in the world.

I called him and spoke the truth. I pointed out things that he did not want to hear. I have a way of doing that when I am feeling brave. I said, "I am worried that your wife divorced you because you cheated. I am worried that you are addicted to AA meetings and you are not getting the right counselling that is needed. Will you ever allow love into your life again? Are all of these concerns relevant?"

Dead silence.

"You have nothing to lose."

More silence.

Finally, he said, "It seems you have formed opinions of me."

I replied emphatically, "Because you don't tell me a damned thing."

We painfully talked it through. He needed to be a gentleman and do the right thing—you do not invite someone to Dallas, then Tampa and Atlanta and then uninvite them!

I figured out that he didn't want to deal with me in Atlanta because his wife and kids lived there. I made it perfectly clear that I did not expect anything from him in Atlanta except to point me in the right direction of the bus depot. One good thing from my quest for the truth was Lee's words, "Telling you the truth, or being more honest, even in an email, is a breakthrough for me. In the past, I would have sabotaged our relationship until it ended."

'Great! Jeez, I am so happy for you.'

At the end of our long phone conversation, I asked him to say one nice thing about me. Huge pause. Finally, he said, "You have a positive energy all around you." Yes, I do. Perhaps I was naïve and maybe idealistic. I would keep dreaming of the impossible. It's much more tantalizing.

Lee finally came to his senses and sent me a hotel confirmation by email. My heart pounded when I read, "king-size bed." Men are strange yet somewhat predictable. I knew he would do the right thing. He even planned to pick me up at the airport. I told myself to not be all over him like a rash. I intended to play it cool and let him come to me, like a tentative horse.

I was flying to Tampa via Toronto but found out from Lee that there were tornado warnings in Atlanta. What does a person say at the end of that conversation? Good luck? Break a leg? Lay low?

The first night in Tampa, we went to Clearwater

for dinner and walked on the beach during an amazing flash lightning storm. I had never seen clouds light up over the ocean like a flash dance before. We held hands, chatted but there was no kissing. The day before I left, I developed a hugely painful and disgusting cold sore on my lip. Maybe it was a sign for limited intimacy on this trip. However, we had plenty of hot sex especially after a day at the beach when your skin was sun-soaked and glistening with bits of soft sand, followed by a cooling shower.

Lee was technically "working" as a big event promotion manager. During the day, I was left to explore Tampa, go to the beach, eat ice cream on the boardwalk, and I enjoyed every minute of it. One night, we had dinner at Jimmy's Fish House. That was following a breakthrough moment on the beach as I watched a ship go by. The sun was setting in a palate of pink and purple splashing above the horizon of the sea. I had an epiphany and realized that I had chosen an unconventional life. Lee had four children and I had none. I chose freedom and it had and has made all the difference. The price to pay — being alone. I felt overwhelming happiness and sadness all at once. It took courage to lead that kind of life. It took courage for me to take that trip. It was risky but I had won, for now. The pirate ship steered towards the sunset. I was that ship floating into the light and the unknown alone and beautiful. I would stay on course and follow the rhythm of my heart and guidance of my soul. I cried softly on that beach for ten minutes and then it was over.

Lee and I had a breakthrough moment during dinner. He was talking in riddles about "co-dependency." I had no idea what he was going on about. I sensed unresolved anger in him. Who was he angry at? His wife? His parents? Himself? I went to the bathroom, looked in the mirror and thought, *'How do I play this one?'* The only thing I could come up with was understanding, love, and acceptance. I walked back to the table and said to him, "I love and accept you just the way you are. I feel like you are holding back on something." Perhaps he found some relief in those words. He paid the bill and I got up to tip the band and have a dance. Another miracle happened. Lee joined me on the dance floor. I was astonished. We danced to *Tainted Love* by Soft Cell. Perhaps a very fitting song.

Saturday morning after another hot sex session, we decided to drive south to Treasure Island Beach and the Salt Rocks. I packed a picnic lunch, towels, and a blanket from our hotel room. It was a smoking hot day so we couldn't wait to get into the ocean. We saw a fetching creature strolling on the beach. He was built like a refrigerator and had skin like leather.

He proudly wore a bubblegum pink thong. He was delightful in the weirdest way possible. There are all kinds of colourful, quirky characters who end up in Florida.

Day three of my adventure ended at Honeymoon Island, a state park with white sand and azure blue waters that reminded me of the Great Barrier Reef. We walked the beach and swam in the warm oceanic waters of the Gulf of Mexico. I saw my first needlefish and ate my first crab roll. At the end of the day, we changed in the rental car and made our way to the airport. We were not on the same flights to Atlanta but were within an hour of each other. I loved the short flight alone in my musing of the last three days.

After my Savannah adventure on my own, I took the bus back to Atlanta and stayed at the hostel on Ponce de Leon Street across from Mary Mac's Tea Room. You know the children's clapping game, "Miss Mary Mack, Mack, Mack…all dressed in black, black, black…" It is a 1945 era institution for locals and tourists alike with Southern comfort food. It has the quintessential flashing red 1940s signage lights on the front of the building. I went straight there for a lunch of southern vittles like fried green tomatoes, cream corn, and a little pot likker soup with cornbread. A youngish black waiter came over to my table and said, "I hope this is not too forward, but I saw you sitting there and thought how cute you are. My daddy told me to seize opportunity so would you like to go to the best blues bar in Atlanta?" I was completely flattered and thought, *'Wow, a backup plan if Lee flakes out on me.'* I told him that I might have a previous engagement. He said, "Well, you have a friend in Atlanta." *Wow, I love this State!*

That night, Lee came through for me. We went out for dinner at a neighbourhood Cuban restaurant near Piedmont Park and Myrtle Street. It was a lovely warm evening with a smiling crescent silver moon shining down on us. I told him stories of Savannah. We talked about key lime and lemon meringue pies. He said, "I like the tart, which could be why I like you." Those words went way over my head so I made him repeat. I said, "Two can play at that game. At least you didn't call me a whore... or ho." He continued to speak in riddles and faint clues of his deeper feelings for me. I was fascinated by it all. I said, "Thank you for taking good care of me," as we embraced in the car. I put his hand over my breast and heart. I was wearing my orange, silky, plunging neckline blouse and Miracle Bra. I must have blown the poor boy's mind with my sensuality. Maybe I was a tart.

In front of the International Hostel, Lee walked me to the front door as a good southern/Canadian gentleman would. We embraced and I kissed him full on the lips for the first time in a week. My lip was almost healed. Everything and everyone needs time to heal. Seeing moments of lightness, I hoped for more. As he walked back to the car, I saluted him and said, "I love you, Lee Robinson." In that moment, I did. However, it was time to fly back to Canada and close that chapter. As Ray Charles sang, I would always have "Georgia on my mind."

Home

Bittersweet.

You would think that after my Savannah adventure, life would have been clear sailing. I wish this were true. How many times does one have to break down before one can break through? I don't know. Perhaps it is a lifelong process until we die.

I was still in love with Lee from Atlanta. I dreamed of him coming back to Canada and staying with me in the condo that I had owned for seventeen years. I was sure that Puddy, my big tabby cat, would love him, too. I imagined meeting him at the airport, driving home and making love all weekend. I had purchased a helicopter ride in the mountains from a silent auction that I happened to be pouring wine at. I seized the opportunity, made a low bid, and won. Imagine what a surprise it would be to drive Lee out to the mountains right up to the helicopter pad and say, "How about a ride?" Unfortunately, none of that happened. Lee had obligations in Atlanta with his four children, job, and he was still in love with his ex-wife. Well, at least we'd had Toronto.

I continued to work as a coordinator for an event management company. My boss, however, was losing money and could no longer pay me twenty-five bucks an hour. My hours were cut, and I worried about making ends meet. I lived on credit and the hope of more clients and more hours. That did not happen, and our business relationship ended in the fall of 2011.

I picked up some hours hosting wine tastings for a few wine agents. The thought of starting over with another low paying job was too much for me to bear. I began to sink slowly but surely — again. Before the worst of it, I managed to pull off another tacky Christmas gift party. I sponsored a family in need and requested on the invitations that guests either donate cash or a gift for the mother and children. I dropped off the gift package to the family's small apartment. A young boy came down the hall with a huge smile on his face. I gave him a laundry basket full of gifts, went back to my car, and cried like a baby. I was overwhelmed with joy and sadness.

In January 2012, I sank further into oblivion. By early March, my neighbour and good friend Ken phoned my parents and said, "She is lying in bed, talking of drinking bleach." I had two choices: a hospital or home. I chose the latter. But, how would I get home? Ken suggested that I take the bus from Calgary to Medicine Hat three hours away. My parents would meet me there. My best friend Mary came over to make a list and help me pack. I was full of anxiety and uncertainty. I took sleeping pills because I had no anti-anxiety pills. I could not escape from depression anxiety.

Ken drove me to the bus station. He left me there to wait. It was not so bad because I managed to talk with the gals at the ticket counter. It was six in the evening. I boarded the bus and was shaking with the movement of the bus on the highway. By ten in the evening, I wondered where the bus would drop passengers off. We end up in a deserted mall parking lot somewhere in Medicine Hat. It was dark, cold, and desolate. I cried in anticipation and fear of seeing my father. Where was he? Was he lost? I looked out the window and saw the familiar Chevrolet alone and waiting. My dad stepped out of the car and hugged me. I cried into his shoulder.

"Are you hungry?" he asked.

"Yes, a little." We drove over to Tim Horton's for a soup and bun. Then, we drove back west several kilometres to the motel where my mother waited. She was worried because Dad had been gone for so long. I embraced her. The beautiful bedroom upstairs in the loft was reserved for me. I had a bath, took a sleeping pill, and laid on the puffy, clean hotel pillows, drifting off into a comforting sleep. I wished that I could have stayed that way forever. It was an impossible dream.

Six weeks later, after doctors, counselling, and self-care in Radville and Weyburn, I found myself driving back to Calgary with my oldest sister Michelle. She had graciously offered to drive me nine hours back home. Deep down, I knew my sister wanted to relieve my parents of the burden. My mother was losing her sight and hearing. My father was losing his patience. It was time to cut the umbilical cord.

Love

*Uncertainty is the fertile ground of pure joy,
creativity, and imagination.*

My journalist friend Jennifer Gray said to me, "You have such a creative flair and gift for helping people to heal and feel loved; to feel joy." I wanted to believe her. I said to myself, "Don't ever forget this."

In the spring of 2012, I decided to have a fresh start—a rebirth, if you will. In April and May, Calgary can be like winter often snowing May long weekend. There were days I felt frigidly cold, constricted, and frozen like ice crystals hanging the air. But, wait for it… a Chinook wind from the west… the temperature will climb twenty degrees Celsius in one day. No wonder we are all nuts in Calgary and Leonardo DiCaprio thought it was a sign of global warming.

I was inspired by the writings and audio cassette tapes of Earl Nightingale given to me by Dad. It is called the Essence of Success with fundamental ideas like creativity, opportunity, and goal setting, the mind, and happiness. His teachings as a 1940s radio broadcaster and writer blew my mind. He used words that I had to look up, quotes of his own and countless inspirational people that I had not heard before. These fascinating principles, in theory, are invaluable but putting them into practice is a different story. Making a living in a boom and bust city that changed with the wind was also another story.

I was moved by a film called *A Dangerous Method* starring Michael Fassbender as Jung and Viggo Mortenson as a fifty-year-old Freud. It was an intense relationship between a Swiss psychiatrist and an Austrian Neurologist. Keira Nightly, as Russian Sabina, barnstormed her way through hysteria in the first fifteen minutes of the film. I didn't believe her. For the remainder of the film, however, she was convincing as a woman suffering from mental illness and sexual dysfunction. Viggo was witty and intelligent as Fassbender's alter ego, friend, and colleague. Fassbender played a gifted psychiatrist flawed simply by being human and falling in love with his patient. He left his wife and used experimental treatments on Sabina that may or may not have been ahead of his time. In the film, he said, "Sometimes you have to do something unforgivable just to go on living." Perhaps he was prophetic to me.

I had an inventory of gratitude in the New Year: a bright red SMART car (only as smart as the person driving it) that spelled freedom; a cat that understood me, maybe; a hiking group that I could go cross-country skiing and hiking in the mountains with; new students in yoga and Pilates at my little Inglewood studio; most importantly, a supportive front row of family and friends. The problem was, I had little money and didn't know what I wanted to do for work. I was on again and off again with sleeping pills to dull my suppressed emotional pain and fear of the future. From experience, I knew that if I settled for a spirit sucking job, I would fall into a tailspin. I always was in flux, fighting off lonely birds.

I found comfort, companionship, and exploration of new vistas with my hiking group. We ventured up to Rockbound Lake near Castle Mountain (it really looks like a castle, but not the Disney kind) twenty kilometres west of Banff. Three hours up, we discovered The Blue Lagoon emerald lake, spectacular rock formations, and a lovely spot for lunch. My closer hiking buddy said to me, "Famous, smart people in the world have sunk to the depths of depression only to break through, crawl out, and find a new spark." Perhaps I was in the process of finding my spark and new ventures by being patient and smart.

I also drummed up the courage to head west to Nelson, British Columbia. I needed to not only test my courage wings out but also connect with my comrade cousin Rob. I left my urban life of worry in my little red sports car with one tank of gas, up and through the winding highways west through the Rocky Mountains. I stopped in Fernie, British Columbia for borscht, gelato, and yack (what is yack?). I even picked up a hitchhiker dude in Salmo that was on his way to a crazy music festival called Shambhala. It was held during the last week of July at the Salmo River Ranch in the West Kootenay mountains near Nelson. It was Canada's premiere Electronic Music Festival with cutting edge artists of all kinds on six themed stages of light, art, music, and dance. Woodstock, USA, eat your heart out. I did not partake as crowds, at that time in my life, gave me anxiety.

The highlight of my trip was floating down the Slocan River with Rob's partner Nick and his two friends, Tom and Billy. We hit rapids, calm pools of water, and sandy beaches. I even discovered my wild and spontaneous side by swinging topless from a tree performing a perfect belly, booby flop. The swimming and healing waters washed away my aches, pains, and worries.

Dearest Rob invited me to spend one more day in Nelson. We had been in the trenches together with a glimpse of sunlight and a future of hope for love, happiness, and purpose. We had walked a mile in each other's shoes, and would likely walk many more.

I drove back to Calgary ready to face my fears

of living alone and finding a new job in Cowtown. I realized that abundance has nothing to do with money. Money was not my business, but truth was. Am I supposed to have more money than I have? Less? I am supposed to have exactly what I have. Isn't that enough?

I had an interview with the owner of Hotel Arts in downtown Calgary. He seemed to be impressed with me because he said, "Lizzie, you could help run this company." He sent off my application to human resources and a week later, they offered me a position as a hostess for the Raw Bar Restaurant. It felt like I was going backwards. A friend said, "Rock this job."

'It is a steppingstone job. Do your best AND be your own best friend.'

I met Don Murray on October twelfth in the early afternoon. He was a general contractor finishing all the electrical work in the owner's restaurant creation called The Yellow Door. He was boyishly cute with a smile of pearly whites from ear to ear. He stopped and flirted with me at the hostess station. He called me "Thin Lizzy" and I courageously asked him out for a drink. He was busy at that moment, so we arranged to meet at my hostess station Friday after work at three in the afternoon. Apparently, he did not show up, or did he? We missed each other by about five minutes. We decided to meet a week later at the Kensington

Pub for a drink and food. He was on time and I was fashionably fifteen minutes late. He looked antsy.

We had a couple of drinks and food that we barely touched. We were very dialled into each other and our conversation. We talked about everything under the sun, including a bit about my past careers, family, and nothing about our present work.

"Do you think freedom is too much of a good thing? Can it be dangerous?" I asked.

He agreed that too much was not good for a person. He said, "I am a loner." He appeared to be as love touched and starved as I.

At one point, he caressed my hand and played with my fingernails. *'Oh jeez, I am in trouble.'* He asked me if I wanted to go back to his house. I agreed as I left my car on the street and climbed up into his truck. On the way, he piped up, "I have a hot tub."

'I am really in trouble.'

I noticed his hedges in the front yard right away. They were on fire with autumn colours. As we walked in the front door, I spotted a black piano in the corner of the living room. *'Trouble, so much trouble.'* Donnie said he played the guitar. I was impressed. Maybe we could play a duet or start a garage band? We went to the kitchen and slow danced to some sweet music. We kissed but I don't know when or how. Do people with sparks flying off their bodies remember the first kiss? We went in the hot tub naked and I lost myself in the soothing hot water and beauty of a fall moon and stars smiling down upon us.

The next morning, he drove me back to my car as big, white, fluffy snowflakes fell. Was it a walk of shame or "fame," as Don would call it? I felt giddy like a schoolgirl and went to work that day carrying around thoughts of the previous night, Don, and the possibility of falling in love.

A few days later, Don texted me, "I miss your wonderful spirit." I had a date with a girlfriend that week and he also said, "The date with your girlfriend almost belittled (good word) our date."

On Sunday, I made banana, chocolate, coconut muffins for him and drove thirty minutes to his place in the northwest, arriving promptly at eight-thirty in the evening. He must have been doing laundry because he piped up with, "Hey, do you want to help me make my bed.?" I gladly helped him, we ended up on the couch cuddling.

"I don't want this to be just a sexual relationship," I said. "I have been to the circus and I don't need to go there again."

"I don't want that either. I really care about you."

He carried me to his bed, and we made love

slowly and tenderly. Tears streamed down my face and I said softly, "Thank you."

For the next six months, I drove over to Don's place time and time again, showing up on his doorstep like a lost puppy. Early in the New Year, I drove over to Don's place and had a strange little car accident in the middle of an intersection. My little Smart car had a dent in the front, and I had slammed on the brake hard. My foot and ankle started to swell and ache. I still managed to stop at the Vietnamese take-out. When I arrived, Donnie was half asleep on the couch watching hockey. I laid beside him. "I had a car accident and my foot is really sore."

"Oh yeah?" he mumbled, barely registering what I had said.

The next day, I could barely walk on it. I couldn't work at Hotel Arts and received disability for a couple of months. I diligently went to physio but was restless without working.

I know I was far from perfect and guess what, so was Donnie. He married in his early twenties, had two beautiful girls, lived in Idaho, worked his ass off, and divorced nine years later. Divorce can be worse than a death in the family. I think a part of Donnie died when he left his daughters to move back to Calgary. He had unresolved anger that he often took out on me by barking and swearing. For the most part, I accepted it and didn't stand up for myself, as I had done throughout my skating career. The good news was that the episodes didn't last long—ten to fifteen minutes, tops—then they would be over.

Within a year, I slowly moved bits of my condo contents into Donnie's house. I did it without asking him, terrified of rejection. Twice a year, Donnie drove down to Idaho to see his daughters. Every time, I cried and had pangs of abandonment feelings in my gut. Donnie was torn between obligation for his family and looking after me and my insecurities.

I was and still am an ambitious wannabe chef and health nut. I made all kinds of delightful dishes and baking depending on the season. I even gave Donnie warm lemon water every morning in bed and packed his lunches with the best multivitamins. These acts of kindness couldn't help but strengthen our relationship. Donnie was and still is a workhorse. I had to force him to take breaks. For the most part, I tried to lead by example, as I had twenty-five years of practicing self-care.

In the spring of 2013, my foot had healed but my heart and soul had a way to go. I lost my job at the Hotel Arts and my little yoga studio in Inglewood. The good news was I was sleeping without medication, had little anxiety, and undying hope for the future. I was a bright light with infinite possibilities.

Breakthrough

Whatever they have done, forgive them.
Whatever you have done, forgive yourself.

On January 27, 2016, I found an outdoor rink in a park two blocks from our home. I found my old skates, wore black tights, jacket, and toque, and trudged in the snow. I had not skated for over twelve years. My heart pounded in my chest. Even my gimped bone spurred foot fit into my skate. I tentatively stepped onto the ice. It was high noon, so the ice was beginning to glisten. I skated in figure eights, stroking around and around, giving my legs time to adjust. My blades were dull, but I stood firm on the edges forwards and backwards. Part of the rink was thin ice with a flakey pie crust topping. I was aware and careful. My legs fatigued after about thirty minutes. I stopped, found my skate guards, and ventured onto the street to find someone to photograph this momentous occasion. There was a nice lady in her car who pulled over for me and was happy to oblige.

"I have not skated in twelve years!" I said enthusiastically.

"Looking good," she replied, taking the shot with my cellphone.

I shared the photo with Geoff and he said, "You have always had the touch."

Oh yes, it was Bell's Let's Talk for Mental Health Day. What could have been better for my mental health?

In the New Year, I was studying Buddhism at the Kadampa Meditation Center. I practiced wise mind, wise speech, heart, and action. I was also fascinated by the four noble truths:

What is the problem?

What is the root cause of the problem?

Is there a solution or cessation to suffering?

How do you put the solution into action?

I asked these questions repeatedly. I practiced loving kindness, one mindfulness, and the art of pausing, relaxing and attending. I listened to John Lennon's *Mind Games* and thought a lot about his simple truths: "Yes is the answer and you know that for sure. Yes, is surrender…ya gotta let it go." I was in the spirit of "yes" and radically raw acceptance.

In February, I had a breakthrough, not breakdown, moment with Donnie. "Do your daughters know about me?"

"Probably not," he shrugged.

"Why, why, why?"

"I don't know."

I knew what it was. "Is it because of what I put you through?"

"Yes."

The flood gates opened. I burst into tears and choked out the words, "Can you ever forgive me?"

He replied simply, "I can forgive you."

I wanted so desperately for him to forgive me for putting through on-again off-again rounds of depression and misery in the first four years of our relationship. Then, I needed to forgive myself and it hurt deep in the pit of my stomach. As John Lennon said, *"Love is the answer, and you know that for sure."*

Breakdown

Arrows in your back
Thorns in your stomach
Pull them out one by one
Forge ahead.

When you attempt suicide, it is the law that you must be hospitalized. I was "committed" to hospital number two on a Friday before the August long weekend of 2016. I was wheeled down a long hall to a one-floor mental health center at Rockyview General Hospital. I had a meeting with a young psychiatric ward fellow who seemed to be in charge. He outlined the rules of the place as I sat there and wondered when I could see a doctor. At the end of it, he gave me a notebook and said, "It is the long weekend so don't expect to see a doctor for four days." If I had a heart condition, stroke, or seizure, would I not see someone right away?

They put me in a separate room with a bed and that was it. Maybe it was a room reserved for crazy people. They also gave me a hospital gown that didn't fit, but I guess it was better than the blood-stained pyjamas from my previous incident at the Foothills hospital. A few doors down, there was a glass fishbowl of a room with a man laying there staring into space. His arm was in a sling and he was strapped down. I walked by and tried not to look. There was a TV room with couches and a dining area. Down the hall, I was surprised to see a door that led to a patio with benches and a small flower garden in the middle. *'Wow, an actual place of refuge.'*

I found a bathroom with a bathtub, had a bath, and ventured to the reception desk. It was about ten in the evening. They gave me Trazodone which I thought was a sleeping pill. I went to my bedroom and tried to sleep. A psychiatric doctor came in and I said, "I think they gave you the wrong medication." We went to the front desk, talked to them, asked me a few questions, and that was it. He seemed like a nice enough doctor, but off he went, as I am sure he wanted to finish his shift before the long weekend.

I slept a little and woke up to a nurse hovering near my bed. "We are moving you to another room."

'Great, another room to endure.' It was a smaller room with three beds. There were two other names on the door but no one else to be seen. I choked down breakfast at eight in the morning and worried about the endless day of anxiety ahead.

There were patients there of all ages, shapes, and

sizes. A young fellow with a blotch of red in his eye watched the movie *Avatar* all day. An old man walked around in a hospital gown and drank instant coffee. A lovely young girl watered the flowers in the outside area and looked like she did not belong in the ward at all. A frail older lady used a walker to get around. The strangest creature was a young Hutterite woman with a huge forehead and tightly bound hair wearing a black, early twentieth century dress. Her husband with a wide-brimmed hat stayed most of the day with her. They kept to themselves.

At one in the afternoon, Doctor Hagen, my psychotherapist, walked in. I was in shock. She greeted me and went straight to the reception desk to talk with nurses. She was dressed professionally, classy yet summery with colourful slim pants and stylish sunglasses. "Why are you here?" I asked.

"Of course I would come to see you." We ventured out to the garden area, sat on a bench, and had a short chat. I told her that I was worried about being kept there for a long time. She reassured me that they wanted people to leave as soon as possible. I wasn't convinced. "Are you sleeping?"

"Sort of, and I think I am on Trazodone."

"That is not a sleeping aid, it is an antidepressant."

Uh oh, I am in trouble.

She left after about thirty minutes and gave the nurse her business card and instructed her to let the doctors know that she had come by.

One hour later, Donnie's mom Joan showed up with a bag of clothes and other necessities. I was happy to see her but also very ashamed. I showed her to the outdoor area, and we sat on a bench in the sun. I looked and felt drugged up. "So, how long are they keeping you here?" she asked.

"I don't know."

She didn't stay long as she looked a bit uncomfortable. I must have looked quite lonely and pathetic when she left.

I didn't sleep for the next three nights. I had panic attacks at two in the morning and begged the nurse to give me something to help my anxiety and sleep. She took my blood pressure. On top of it all, I got my period and had wicked cramps. They gave me Advil. Joan brought me sanitary napkins one day and a nail care kit. Thank god for mothers.

I was allowed low dosage anti-psychotic drugs which made me even more anxious and jittery. My whole body shook from the inside out and once again I begged a young nurse to find me a doctor. She couldn't help me with that. Instead, she tried relaxation techniques. Nothing worked and I said, "I'm not going to make it." She didn't seem to get it and left the room.

One night, I found the movie *Seabiscuit* on DVD and tried to watch it. I felt nothing. An older fella sat on the couch and said, "Did you know that they used four different horses for the racing scenes?" I didn't know that. I learned something that day. All I wanted was to waste time until I could hide in bed.

My roommates were nice enough and kept to themselves. One girl had had a misunderstanding with her psychiatrist and the police had arrived at her house, escorting her to the hospital. She also had a baby. Her partner came to visit, and she changed the baby on her bed. I felt nothing. The only thing I felt was envy as she slept through the night, apparently on lithium. I tossed and turned on a bed that curved the wrong way and on flat hospital pillows. Every hour, a nurse would shine a flashlight in. It was a cruel reminder of each passing hour of insomnia. I wanted to scream at her to leave us the bloody hell alone. I didn't say a word. I went to the bathroom often as a broken light above me flickered on and off. My other roommate snored away and wandered around in a daze for most of the day.

One girl who looked about seventeen years old played the cello. She played in her room every day and once out in the outdoor space. I closed my eyes and let the sad sounds of the cello wash over me. I wondered how a girl who played such beautiful music could end up in a place like this. A lovely long-haired, olive-skinned woman from Fiji, I believe, talked all the time. She told me she had been gang-raped and I had no clue how long she had been in the hospital or even if she was telling the truth. She did tell me to not accept the drugs they gave me and to drink a lot of water. I was constantly drinking water and sucking on ice cubes. She had a crying fit breakdown in her room, wailing away for about twenty minutes. A nurse finally went in to check on her. I thought crying was much better than being in a drug-like zombie state.

Tuesday morning, a large group of doctors showed up. I was assigned to a male psychiatrist and waited patiently to see him. I drank peppermint tea and nervously wandered from one spot to another. By noon, he saw me, and we sat at a small table next to a window. I explained to him how I had not slept in three days and didn't want the Trazadone at all. He listened, asked me a few stock psychiatric questions, and prescribed low dosage anti-anxiety pills and Zopiclone for sleep. Thank God. I immediately went to the reception desk nurse and got an anti-anxiety pill and laid on my bed. *'I am going to sleep and get out of here.'*

That night, I was given my Zopiclone and slept through with wild dreams about my friends Mary and Steve. I knew that I had slept well because of the REM sleep. I felt like a different person. I had spoken to Donnie once, telling him that I couldn't stay in the hospital much longer. He was probably still in shock over my suicidal tendencies yet grateful that his mom was close to the Rockyview Hospital for visits and to bring me stuff.

My psychiatrist arranged for a meeting with him and myself the next morning. He had mentioned a course at the hospital that he taught that involved coping with depression. I had no intention of ever going back to that hospital and thought in the back of my mind that I would agree to attend if it meant releasing me. Donnie came in the middle of work and I met him in the lobby. I prepped him to say exactly what the doctor wanted to hear. The meeting lasted fifteen minutes and I was officially released. I grabbed a few garbage bags full of stuff from my room. A nurse emptied my locker with the only thing of value—my cell phone. My jewelry had been lost at the Foothills hospital five days previously. Donnie drove me home in silence. I had put him through hell. I had been through my own hell. How could he ever forgive me? How could I ever forgive myself?

Misery

I am not afraid of death.
Annihilation of the living heart & soul,
Worse.

From the fall of 2016 to 2019, I was in a state of oblivion. I had a series of spirit sucking jobs, isolated from family and friends, and self-medicated with clonazepam—low dosage valium. When I ran out of that, I got into numbing myself with Gravol. I made myself sick to the stomach and threw up several times. I stayed in bed for half of the day with a facecloth on my forehead and the curtains drawn. When I finally got up, I watched the news for hours, got angry, bored, and more despondent. Donnie didn't know what to do with me.

I had been seeing Doctor Nora Hagen, a psychotherapist in Cochrane. She was good but the drive, plus ninety minutes of intense therapy, was challenging and emotionally exhausting. I continued to see her, took some notes, but was spiralling. I felt guilty for not working. Nora said, "Healing is your most important job at the moment." I wanted to believe her. She also said, "Have wonder about the day, not worry." How could I have wonder about anything when I was dead inside? I wrote down affirmations like, "I always deserve compassion, not judgement. I am precious simply because I exist. My worth is not dependent on a job or achievement. I deserve to feel joy. I am a beautiful, creative human being." I wanted to believe myself. I thought about Owen Wilson in the film *Darjeeling Limited*. His face was covered with bandages. He stood in front of the mirror somewhere in India with his two brothers, removed the bandages, saw the wounds, and said, "Maybe I need a little more time to heal."

Dr. Hagen told me that Carrie Fisher was bipolar and very vocal about it. She also had substance abuse issues and was an alcoholic. She came from a very dysfunctional Hollywood family, but where did she go off course? Fisher died from a cardiac arrest in 2016 at the age of sixty. I didn't care about Princess Leia in *Star Wars*. I saw a funny, vulnerable, and honest woman with a mental illness. I felt her pain and courage. I wanted to be courageous and my pain to end.

I spoke to my dad in the spring of 2019 and he told me my mom was sad. I can take my own sadness and grief, but I just couldn't bear my mom's. Was she lonely, isolated, or depressed? How would I know? How do I accept that with an open heart? Should I write to her? What would I say other than small talk? Questions with no answers.

I tried a cashier job at Community Natural Foods. It was stressful and hard work. I wasn't fast enough and couldn't remember all the silly codes that made no sense whatsoever. *'If I have to pack one more grocery bag for people, I am going to kill myself.'* I lasted two weeks and then was let go. I was sad and relieved. I had been saved from staying with,in the lines like a mindless robot.

I realized that there is no cure for mental illness. How much can a person bear? In September, I attempted suicide for the third time. I went into Donnie's new Toyota car, found a garden hose, and placed it in the muffler, then through a window. I waited and longed for peace. *'Everyone has the right to choose when to die.'* I laid in the front seat for about thirty minutes. Nothing happened. What saved me was a newer car with fewer carbon emissions.

I had left Mary a message before my attempt. I had no idea what I said. I gave up with the car and left the garage with my blanket in hand. Cops were waiting for me outside. I lied to them, saying god knows what so I wouldn't be taken to another hospital. Mary was furious with me. I couldn't blame her. Donnie was beside himself. The police requested a social worker to come and see me the next day. A couple of nice ladies stopped by and spoke with me for about an hour. I was angry. I described to them my experience with bipolar disorder and my hospitalizations. I told them that if you tell doctors this diagnosis, they hand out anti-psychotics like candy. I was never psychotic! I experienced Akathisia which is numbing and shaking from the inside out. I felt crazy and couldn't sit still. I found out about this horrible side effect from watching a Netflix series called *Paranoid*. I knew exactly how the British cop felt when he walked into a German pharmaceutical company, stared at a plastic statue of Jesus filled with colourful pills, and slammed it against the floor. The pills scattered everywhere. Security escorted him out of the building.

Fuck doctors and hospital psychiatrists! Damn them all. I had been silent for years and then I completely lost it. I felt like Red Pollard, the jockey in *Seabiscuit*, abandoned by his family in the great depression, brewing with anger, and fighting for his life. Or better yet, Seabiscuit alone in a barn stall kicking the wood and dying to run free. I asked myself, *'Lizzie, why are you so angry?'*

As a child, I had felt like I had been punished for having a gift. I knew that my parents really had only one choice—they had to send me away so I could shine for all of the world to see. The thirty miles to Weyburn and back again would play in my mind for the rest of my life.

I said to my dad, "I am not afraid of death."

"I am not afraid of death either."

"I am more afraid of being dead inside whilst I am living."

ACT III

Help

Are dreams really
"Impossible. Improbable. Inevitable?"

"Mary, you are a bright light at the end of a very dark tunnel."

"When did you think you were not worthy of my love and friendship?" she asked.

"When I was thirteen and thought I had to go it

alone. I kept myself busy so I wouldn't have to feel the loneliness, sadness, frustration, anger, resentment, shame, and fear of never being good enough."

Mary hooked me up with a counsellor and life coach named Lisa Hogue in the fall of 2019. She lived in Lethbridge and we had ninety-minute to two-hour phone conversations. I bought a Sony recorder and started recording our sessions, and I always wrote while we talked so I could remember everything we said. Her voice was soothing, her words were kind, and compassionate. I liked her immediately.

She suggested I read *Untethered Soul* by Michael A. Singer. It was and still is the most powerful book I have read in years. I read a chapter every night before I went to bed thinking his soulful words would sink into my subconsciousness. Chapters like *The Voice Inside Your Head*, *The Lucid Self*, *Let Go Now or Fall*, and *Removing Your Inner Thorn* became covered with notes in the margins. What an amazing book.

Lisa had powerful words of her own to share with me. Phrases like, "be a lighthouse, show the way, this gig is up, and looking for approval outside of yourself is a trap" come to mind. She taught me to open my heart again which had been closed for many years. With each thorn I removed from my side, back, and heart, I felt freedom. Did it hurt like hell? You bet it did. However, it didn't last.

I learned that I couldn't carry the burden of my family anymore. My mom, dad, and siblings' pain was not mine—neither were their frustration, resentment, or anger. I also had a voice and was no longer afraid to speak my truth. I knew that I was a writer and artist. I had to tell my story and I had absolutely nothing to lose. If anyone questioned this, I let it go immediately and turned to those who were supportive—Donnie, Lisa, Mary, a few choice friends, and my editor.

I had lucid dreams of wanting to throw up and had this awful gunk in my throat. It was stuck and wouldn't come out. I woke up half asleep, ran to the fridge, and drank ginger ale to wash the crap out. I also had anger stuck in my gut. I had dreams of being stabbed in the stomach. I ran and pulled out whatever was stuck there. I was subconsciously releasing garbage. I said to myself, "Mom and Dad, I forgive you. Coaches and teachers, I forgive you. Doctors and psychiatrists, I forgive you. And, most importantly, Lizzie, I forgive you." Oh yes, "Donnie, please forgive me."

I realized that I was not put on this earth to be cute, clever, or judgmental of anyone, including myself. My job is to love and be loved. The rest is just details. As David Bowie said, "The really important thing is to look after your family; pop culture is just a bonus." However, he was a husband and father at that point in his life. I am certain he enjoyed fame and fortune, too.

Donnie stood by me during all of this. He was supportive of my sessions with Lisa which were at times emotionally draining. He continued to work hard as a master electrician, providing us with an income while I healed my life. Without him, I could never have finished this book. I tried to be a lighthouse every day, knowing that anger and blame were in the past.

At Christmas, I sent a beautiful eight-by-ten-inch colour photo of our eighty-year-old mom and dad embracing in their garden to all my siblings. Donnie left for Idaho to visit his daughters and I was left alone to be tested again. Lisa told me that Christmas was a difficult time for most families. She and her husband took off to Mexico every year. Once again, I had pangs of abandonment feelings in my gut. Donnie was gone for a whole week, so I planned to cross-country ski with my friend Cynthia. I spent a lot of time staring at the fake fireplace on television. I dared to drive twenty kilometres south in Calgary to Mary and Steve's home. Mary brought in a big box and placed it in front of me. I opened it and found an envelope with a Charlie Brown Christmas card and a thousand dollars cash. I was flabbergasted. Steve performed a Christmas concert every year in Inglewood and at the end, the band passed around a hat for folks in need. I couldn't believe they chose me. I had hope for the New Year.

Epiphany

Academy Awards Seizure

In 2019, I did two difficult things, a process that would change everything. One is I filed for bankruptcy and the other was applying for AISH. (Alberta Income for The Severely Handicapped). I had shame surrounding insolvency and disability. Is mental illness a disability? You bet it is. I didn't even know AISH existed until a volunteer fellow from Edmonton who filed my income taxes for me suggested it. There was a ten-page form to fill out plus letters from my psychiatrist and doctor. I wrote them a personal letter as well, just for good measure. It took nine months to get out of bankruptcy and about the same time for AISH to reply. In January 2020, AISH accepted my application and I was scheduled to meet a social worker in the first week of February.

I was still having trouble sleeping and when I did, there were disturbing dreams in my head. I must have been in a process of purging. I also decided that I was going to do some research for this book, including recording my dad by telephone and talking to my eldest sister about Mom. I emailed Michelle, my eldest sister, in early February and asked her if it would be all right if I sent her some questions for her to answer on her own time. She agreed. About a week later, she said she was busy. She completely blew me off and turned on me. I was devastated. I wrote to her and said, "If the questions were difficult, I apologize." She made it truly clear that she didn't want any kind of relationship with me and said some horrible, very untrue things. I tried desperately to plead my case but to no avail. She became angrier and I gave up.

I began eating marijuana gummies with THC in them and went completely off my rocker. I tried to go for groceries and fell at the doorway in a crumpled mess. I had also run out of anti-anxiety medication, which led to four days of insomnia. I was in deep trouble again. On February 8th, the Friday before Academy Awards Sunday, I had to somehow make it to my AISH appointment. I phoned Mary and she talked me through it. She told me to give myself plenty of time, brush my teeth, and splash water on my face. I had not slept for three nights, was full of anxiety, and doubted that I could ever make the meeting twenty kilometres away. I gathered every ounce of courage I could muster and went to my car. I had one errand to run which was getting a copy of my bank statements. There was an accident a few blocks away. I saw police everywhere, panicked and drove through a police stop. A frantic policeman waved me over to the side of the road. He was livid. I blurted out, "I have a mental illness, have not slept and have to get to AISH for an appointment."

"Well," he said, "you shouldn't be driving." In retrospect, he was right. *'I am attracting shit.*

I waited for fifteen minutes while he wrote out a ticket. It seemed like an eternity. He had calmed down and was a little kinder to me and sent me on my way. I made it to the bank and then to AISH. My social worker was so kind and compassionate. We went through the forms as I wrote notes in the margins to help with my memory. I phoned Mary and told her that I made it.

Another night of insomnia went by and I knew that I was going to end up in the hospital. Donnie was very worried about me. Sunday afternoon, I tried to watch the Academy Awards. Brad Pitt was making an acceptance speech for best-supporting actor in a Quentin Tarantino movie called *Once Upon a Time in Hollywood*. I saw a flash of light off the screen and then a rainbow of colours. The next thing I remember was a first responder dude crouched over me asking me questions I couldn't answer. I was laying on the couch and Donnie was sitting by my feet. Apparently, the EMS guy asked me what year it was. I said,

"Aaahhhh... 2004." It took me at least half an hour to become coherent. Somehow, they got me into an ambulance. Donnie was not far behind as we made our way to the Foothills hospital.

I was taken care of very well. The doctors and nurses take seizures very seriously. They performed all kinds of tests on me and asked a lot of questions. Donnie was right beside the bed, waiting with me patiently and calmly. They gave me a warm blanket and ice water to sip on. It was two in the morning when they sent me home. I made sure that the doctor gave me Zopiclone so I could sleep that night—and I did.

The next day, Donnie told me his side of the story. He was watching the Academy Awards with me and suddenly I was convulsing and making weird sucking noises. Donnie had first aid training, so he knew that it was a seizure. He let me go through it and made sure I was safe. He held me on his chest and gently lowered me to the rug. He put me in a recovery position and called 911. He was my hero.

When people ask me about this experience, I say simply, "It was the perfect storm." From that day forward, my whole being changed. *'This was a one-time deal and I am never going to put Donnie though that again.'* With each passing day, I became stronger in body and mind. I exponentially grew in so many ways.

A week later, Donnie and I watched *Jo Jo Rabbit* — the best movie of the year in my mind. I remember the young boy and girl dancing and singing on the street to *Heroes* by David Bowie. They were Donnie and me, "just for one day."

I had a night scare. I dreamt that a girl stabbed me in the stomach. I put my hand over the wound to stop the bleeding. My intestines were falling out. I tried to get someone to call an ambulance. No one helped. I was lost in a toxic ghetto part of a city. I couldn't escape. I was running and holding in my guts at the same time. I pushed them back in. Then, it became a lucid dream. Through my third eye, I watched myself. In my dream, I thought, *'Enough.'* Then, it was over.

Donnie told me the next morning, "You were yelling and screaming in your sleep."

'This was my dream and I am going to interpret in my own way.' It was a fight to let go of the crap that didn't serve me anymore and live.

Hope & Joy

When you have hope, you carry the burden of pain.

When you let go of pain, you are left with joy.

Now I skip through the days with a lightness in my step and heart. It is summer and our garden is abundantly beautiful. I fell in love with myself and then Donnie and then the world. After four months of COVID and pandemic, I have completed a book. I have made peace with all that burdened me. In March, I thought to myself, *'This is it; this is your chance.'* I seized the opportunity and ran with it.

Seabiscuit died on May 17th (my birthday), 1947 likely from a heart attack. His heart must have burst. That was why he could be so small and run so fast. "It is not in his legs; it is in his heart." Am I a reincarnation of Seabiscuit? Maybe. Are we not just recycled energy repeatedly?

The final race in the movie gets me every time. Seabiscuit falls back from the pack. Pollard struggles with his leg in the stirrup. The music softens. They both find their legs and catch up to a horse and rider that they know. Wolf, the jockey, said, "Have a nice ride, Johnny." The music swells. Seabiscuit passes each horse one by one, weaving his way through openings in the pack. He rounds the last corner with a burst of energy. In slow motion, they cross the finish line and beyond into the light. "You don't throw a whole life away just because you are banged up a little."

What will I take with me into the darkness of death? I will take with me the fresh smell of pond ice in the winter; gentle snowflakes on my face; gliding and floating above the ice; my mom and dad's sad and hopeful eyes. In the meantime, I will wait for the next sad song to come along—and it will—but I am ready. I am waiting for winter.

About the Author

Photo Credit: Janet Pliszka of Visual Hues Photography

Elizabeth (Lizzie) Prost lives in Calgary, Alberta, Canada with her guy Donnie. She adores throwing theme parties and drinking cocktails in her garden. She has a winter garden, too.

Connect with Elizabeth online:

www.elizabethprost.com
Facebook.com/elizabethprostauthor
Youtube.com/elizabeth prost

Forthcoming Titles from Elizabeth A. Prost

Coming in 2021

Break Through Not Down
A Mental Health Handbook with Illustrations

CPSIA information can be obtained
at www.ICGtesting.com
Printed in the USA
BVHW092320131022
649416BV00005B/21